Family Circle

BIG BOOK OF
Christmas

GREAT HOLIDAY RECIPES, GIFTS AND DECORATING IDEAS

A LEISURE ARTS PUBLICATION

Family Circle
BIG BOOK OF
christmas

LEISURE ARTS
Vice President and Editor-at-Large: Anne Van Wagner Childs
Vice President and Editor-in-Chief: Sandra Graham Case
Editorial Director: Susan Frantz Wiles
Publications Director: Susan White Sullivan
Design Director: Cyndi Hansen
Creative Art Director: Gloria Bearden
Photography Director: Karen Hall
Art Operations Director: Jeff Curtis

FAMILY CIRCLE
Editor-in-Chief: Susan Kelliher Ungaro
Executive Editor: Barbara Winkler
Foods Director: Peggy Katalinich
How-To's Editor: Kathryn Rubinstein

G+J USA PUBLISHING
Books & Licensing Director: Tammy Palazzo
Books & Licensing Manager: Carla Clark
Books & Licensing Assistant: Deirdre Stieglitz

LEISURE ARTS EDITORIAL STAFF

EDITORIAL
Managing Editors: Suzie Puckett and Alan Caudle
Senior Associate Editor: Susan McManus Johnson
Associate Editors: Jennifer Riley and Darla Kelsay

TECHNICAL
Senior Editor: Sherry T. O'Connor
Copy Editor: Carol McElroy

FOODS
Foods Editor: Jane Kenner Prather

DESIGN
Designers: Cherece Athy, Polly Tullis Browning, Diana Sanders Cates, Peggy Elliott Cunningham, Anne Pulliam Stocks, Linda Diehl Tiano, and Becky Werle
Executive Assistant: Lucy Beaudry

ART
Art Director: Mark Hawkins
Senior Production Artist: Mark R. Potter
Production Artist: Elaine Barry
Photographer: Russell Ganser
Photography Stylists: Tiffany Huffman and Janna Laughlin
Publishing Systems Administrator: Becky Riddle
Publishing Systems Assistants: Myra S. Means and Chris Wertenberger

PROMOTIONS
Associate Editor: Steven M. Cooper
Designer: Dale Rowett
Graphic Artist: Deborah Kelly

LEISURE ARTS BUSINESS STAFF

Publisher: Rick Barton
Vice President, Finance: Tom Siebenmorgen
Director of Corporate Planning and Development: Laticia Mull Cornett
Vice President, Retail Marketing: Bob Humphrey
Vice President, Sales: Ray Shelgosh

Vice President, National Accounts: Pam Stebbins
Director of Sales and Services: Margaret Sweetin
Vice President, Operations: Jim Dittrich
Comptroller, Operations: Rob Thieme
Retail Customer Service Manager: Wanda Price
Print Production Manager: Fred F. Pruss

Copyright © 2001 by Leisure Arts, Inc., 5701 Ranch Drive, Little Rock, Arkansas 72223-9633. Visit our Web site at **www.leisurearts.com**. Copyright © 2001 by G+J USA Publishing, 375 Lexington Avenue, New York, New York 10017-5514, **www.familycircle.com**. All rights reserved. No part of this book may be reproduced in any form or by any means without the prior written permission of the publisher, except for brief quotations in reviews appearing in magazines or newspapers. We have made every effort to ensure that these recipes and instructions are accurate and complete. We cannot, however, be responsible for human error, typographical mistakes, or variations in individual work. Made in the United States of America.

Library of Congress Catalog Number 98-66514
Hardcover ISBN 1-57486-241-3
Softcover ISBN 1-57486-242-1

10 9 8 7 6 5 4 3 2 1

TIDINGS OF
comfort AND joy

One of my favorite things about the holiday season is the flood of happy memories that accompanies it. I love to reflect on long-ago Christmases with my parents, my sister and four brothers, revisit the sound of my three kids pleading to go see what Santa stashed under the tree (at 5 AM!) and recall Christmas Eve 25 years ago when my husband proposed by tucking a diamond ring in the pocket of a cardigan sweater he gave me.

In that spirit, it's a pleasure to present this colorful, idea-packed volume to help you create celebrations you'll look back on year after year. It's a book I'm confident you'll turn to again and again, because everything you need is included: gorgeous yet do-able decorating ideas and how-to's, clever wrapping hints, scrumptious meals and more.

Thumb through and you'll see the possibilities are endless! Transform your home into a Winter Wonderland with silver stockings and snowflake motifs. Stitch a tree skirt or craft homemade ornaments that will become treasured family keepsakes. Fashion fetching flower arrangements. Set a marvelous mood with candles of all shapes and sizes. Make easy one-of-a-kind gifts, from pillows to picture frames. And that's just the beginning.

Eat, drink and be merry, so the saying goes. These pages offer a trove of terrific recipes to incorporate into your repertoire, including tasty casseroles and irresistible finger foods. There's an array of divine desserts, too, as well as traditional party libations such as eggnog. If you're so inclined, check out the chapter of goodies to give as gifts; you'll delight your neighbors or co-workers. Everything looks spectacular and tastes sublime.

May this *Family Circle Big Book of Christmas* spark joyful anticipation of this and future holidays.

Susan Ungaro

Susan Ungaro
Editor-in-Chief, Family Circle

contents

TO: SANTA North Pole

winter
WONDERLAND

be inspired by the crystalline beauty and snowy splendor of the season. Set the scene with frosty silvers, brilliant blues and clear-as-ice accents. Listen carefully…you can hear sleigh bells ringing.

How-To's on page 12

This year, catch our snowflakes and hold them in your hand, rope our stars and ring them round your tree. All of the pieces come together in one moment of magic. The pièce de résistance: our snowflake star, perched in its proper place, crowning a twinkling tabletop tannenbaum. Also gracing the tree: chenille snowballs, pipe cleaner snowflakes, a mirror garland and a satin tree skirt.

How-To's on page 116

A trio of Victorian stockings (below) are hung by the chimney with care, not to mention pizzazz. Gussied up in silk and satin and dangling from silvery ribbons, they're magnificent to behold. The presents under the tabletop tree, agleam with shining bows, paper diamonds and metallic pom-poms (opposite, top), are almost too pretty to open — almost. Dream by the fire as you cuddle under our appliquéd throw (opposite, bottom).

MISTY-GRAY STOCKING

You need: 1/2 yd gray satin fabric; 1/8 yd lavender crinkle satin fabric; 1/2 yd lavender beaded trim; 2/3 yd of 7/8"W lavender satin ribbon.

Cutting: Enlarge patterns (page 117). From gray satin, cut two stocking pieces for front and back. From lavender satin, cut two cuffs.

Sewing: *All stitching is done in 1/2" seams, with right sides facing and raw edges even, unless noted.* Stitch stocking front to back, leaving upper edge open. Pin trim to right side along one long edge of one cuff section; stitch close to edge using zipper foot. Stitch cuff sections together along short ends and trimmed long edge. Trim seams; turn right side out. Stitch cuff to upper edge of stocking, with right side of cuff facing wrong side of stocking, so cuff ends overlap slightly at center front. Turn right side out. Turn down cuff.

Finishing: Cut a 7" length of ribbon. Fold ribbon in half crosswise; stitch ends together. Stitch ends inside upper back edge of stocking to make hanging loop. Tie remainder of ribbon in bow around hanging loop; trim ends.

ICE-BLUE STOCKING

You need: 1/2 yd ice-blue reversible satin fabric; 1/2 yd matching sequin trim; 1/2 yd wired silver ribbon.

Cutting: Enlarge pattern (page 117). From satin, cut two stocking pieces for front and back (lighter side is right side), one cuff (darker side is right side) and one 2 1/2" x 7" piece for hanging loop.

Sewing: *All stitching is done in 1/2" seams, with right sides facing and raw edges even, unless noted.* Stitch stocking front to back, leaving upper edge open. Fold cuff in half crosswise; stitch short ends together. Turn under 1/2" on lower edge of cuff; press. Slip cuff over upper edge of stocking, with both pieces wrong side out and seams aligned. Stitch cuff to upper edge of stocking. Turn right side out. Turn down cuff. Pin trim along lower edge of cuff; slip-stitch close to both edges of trim.

Finishing: Stitch long edges of loop piece together. Turn right side out. Fold loop in half crosswise; stitch ends together. Stitch ends inside upper back edge of stocking to make hanging loop. Knot ribbon loosely around hanging loop.

How-To's continued on page 116

APPLIQUÉD NAPKINS

You need (for four 12" square napkins): $^1/_2$ yd of 54"W blue taffeta; pinking shears; $^3/_8$"W fusible hem tape; large fusible white fabric snowflakes.

Assembling: Cut four 13" squares of fabric. Turn under $^1/_2$" on raw edges; press. Trim raw edges with pinking shears; cut corners diagonally $^1/_2$" past folds. Cut four 12" pieces of fusible tape for each napkin; slip pieces between hem folds. Press to hem napkins. Cut out and place a snowflake on each napkin. Following manufacturer's directions, fuse snowflakes onto napkins.

FONDANT SNOWFLAKES AND PLACE CARD

You need: Prepared rolled fondant; snowflake and star cookie cutters; paring knife; piping gel (for place card).

Preparing: Following package instructions, roll out fondant and cut out using cookie cutters; use knife to make additional designs on cutouts. Allow to set. To make place card, use piping gel to write guest's name on snowflake.

How-To's continued on page 116

Graceful groupings (opposite) *define a scene-stealing tableau. Clockwise from top left: A snowflake place mat of tin is as beautiful as the real thing. Star garland makes a dramatic focal point when draped over a silver-leaf mirror stamped with flakes. An edible fondant place card sits atop lovely appliquéd napkins. Decorate a cake with a flurry of fondant snowflakes.*

MINI SKATES

You need (for 1 pair of skates):
4" x 16" piece of white polished cotton fabric; thin cardboard; fiberfill stuffing; black embroidery floss; paintbrush; metallic silver acrylic paint; crafts glue.

Cutting: Use full-size patterns (page 118). From cotton, cut four front/back sections. From cardboard, cut two blades and two bases.

Sewing: Pin two sections together, right sides facing and raw edges even; stitch in 1/4" seam, leaving upper edge open. Turn right side out. Turn under 1/4" on upper edge; stitch close to fold to hem skate. Make other skate in same manner. Stuff each skate about three-quarters full. Thread needle with three strands of floss; stitch up front of each skate in crisscross pattern, leaving long floss ends at top to make laces. Make a knot at each end of lace. Tie laces in a bow.

Making blades: Paint blades and bases; let dry. Glue blade in center of each base; let dry. Glue base to bottom of each skate; let dry.

Finishing: Make stitch at upper back of each skate with ends of 10" piece of floss to join skates into one ornament.

VICTORIAN SKATER

You need: Fabrics – 1/4 yd blue velvet; remnants of muslin and white polished cotton; 6" square of lightweight cardboard; remnant of yarn in desired hair color; fabric glue; 2 chenille stems; small amount of fiberfill stuffing; fine-point permanent black marker; pink chalk pencil; 1/2 yd each of silver sequin trim and wired silver braid trim; small paintbrush; metallic silver acrylic paint; crafts knife; silver thread.

Cutting: Use full-size patterns (page 119). From cardboard, cut two skate blades, two skate bases and one bodice along inner line. From velvet, cut one bodice along outer line, one 14" x 4 1/2"

skirt, one 8" x 1 1/4" arm section, one 2" x 4" muff and one 1" circle for hat. From muslin, cut one head front and two head backs. From polished cotton, cut four leg/skate sections.

Assembling bodice: Sew running stitches 1/4" from edges of velvet bodice. Place small amount of stuffing on bodice cardboard. Place bodice velvet on top, right sides up; wrap velvet edges to wrong side, pulling thread to gather. Glue in place, overlapping edges.

Making skirt: *All stitching is done in 1/4" seams, with right sides facing and raw edges even, unless noted.* Turn under 1/4" on one long edge of skirt; sew running stitches close to edge. Do not cut thread. Turn under 1/2" on other long edge; stitch close to fold to hem skirt. Pull up gathering stitches, with ends in back of bodice; knot threads together and glue skirt edges.

Head: Stitch head back sections together, leaving 1" opening in center. Stitch head front to back. Clip curves; turn right side out. Stuff lightly; slip-

stitch opening closed. Using marker, draw features, referring to photograph (page 6). Using chalk pencil, draw cheeks. Glue yarn to head for hair; trim ends.

Legs/skates: Stitch each pair of leg sections together, leaving upper edges open. Trim seams; turn right side out. Stuff firmly, stopping in middle of leg. Cut two 3" pieces of chenille stem; insert each into a leg. Glue or hand-stitch upper edges closed. Use marker to draw lines on skates for laces.

Arm: Cut an 8" piece of chenille stem; coat with glue and place near one long edge of arm section. Roll velvet, right side out, around chenille stem, adding glue as needed.

Assembling: Glue each leg to bottom of bodice, under skirt. Glue arm to center back of body. Bring "hands" to front and glue together. Glue sequin trim around neck and down front of dress. Glue head to body. Cut two 2 1/2" lengths of braid trim for "feathers." Glue feathers to head; glue hat over feathers. Glue braid trim along each long edge of muff. Roll muff around arms, covering hands; glue edges together.

Finishing: Paint skate blades and bases silver; let dry. Using crafts knife, cut slits where indicated on bases. Insert tabs on each blade through base. Glue blades to bottom of feet. Cut 10" of silver thread; sew through back of head and knot ends to make hanging loop.

"ETCHED" SNOWFLAKE GLASSES

You need: Assorted stemmed glasses; permanent spray adhesive; fusible white fabric snowflakes in assorted sizes.

Decorating: Wash and dry glasses. Remove snowflakes from backing; spray back of each snowflake with adhesive. Press onto glasses as desired, smoothing from center out to remove any air bubbles.

Note: Hand-wash glasses.

*I*t's the simple things that are most enchanting and that cast an indelible spell. *The translucent delicacy of etched glasses (below) echoes the icy wintertime landscape. The dainty stemware was found at a flea market, then spangled with snowy impressions. String a pair of mini skates (opposite) from a mantel for a tender turn-of-the-century touch.*

WINNING
window boxes

IMPROVE THE VIEW, INSIDE AND OUT, WITH
EASY-ON-YOU TABLEAUX! "WINTERIZE" WINDOW
BOXES WITH BABY EVERGREENS AND STORE-BOUGHT
TRIMMINGS. FORCE-BLOOM PAPERWHITES INSIDE A
PICKET FENCE. HANG A DRIPLESS TAPER ABOVE A
WHITEWASHED BOX OF TALLOW BERRIES AND
CYPRESS. OR CRAFT WONDERFUL WINDOW
ACCENTS FROM CHICKEN WIRE OR DECORATIVE
BIRDHOUSES. IT'S BEGINNING TO LOOK
A LOT LIKE CHRISTMAS!

How-To's on page 120

HAPPY HUES

GAUZY TREE SKIRT

Note: *Tree skirt consists of a large bordered square (48") topped by a small bordered square (36").*

You need: 42"W sheer fabric – 3⅞ yds green, 3½ yds gold.

Cutting fabric for large square: *Green* – Cut one 41" x 41" square (skirt) and one 10" x 10" square (facing). Cut a 5" dia hole in center of facing. Cut two 2"W x 54"L bias strips (ties), pieced as needed. *Gold* – Cut eight 5"W x 51"L strips, following lengthwise grain of fabric.

Cutting fabric for small square: *Gold* – Cut one 31" x 31" square (skirt) and one 10" x 10" square (facing). Cut a 5" dia hole in center of facing. Cut two 2"W x 45"L bias strips (ties), pieced as needed.

Green – Cut eight 4"W x 39"L strips, following lengthwise grain of fabric.

Stitching facing to each skirt square: With right sides facing and corners aligned, pin facing to center of skirt square. Stitch ½" from circle opening. Following cut edge, trim ½" from stitching, cutting a hole in center of skirt. Clip seam allowance every ½" up to the stitching line. Turn facing to

Bring the tree to life with a rainbow of extra-brilliant balls (opposite) painted in lush colors. For a soft foil, make our green and gold tree skirt. Give your tree star power with exciting wooden ornaments (above) embellished with beads and sequins.

deck your **home** in shimmering jewel tones this year and dazzle your **family** and friends with a celebration fit for royalty. Merry up the simplest trims with shining **ribbons**, glitzy beads and brilliant blooms. The vibrant hues add **splashes** of rich color wherever they're displayed.

wrong side of skirt; press. Press under ½" on each straight edge of facing; topstitch to skirt.

Adding border to each skirt: Right sides facing, long edges even, center one border strip on one edge of skirt. Use a ½" seam and sew border to skirt, leaving ½" unstitched at each end. Repeat with remaining border strips. At each corner, press and pin each pair of border ends to create a diagonal (mitered) corner. Stitch along pressing lines. Trim excess fabric, leaving a ½" seam allowance. Press mitered seam open. Press borders flat.

Finishing border: Press under ½" on raw edge of skirt border. Fold each border in half to wrong side of skirt, matching pressed edge to stitching line; pin. Topstitch through all layers.

Making ties: Press each bias strip in half lengthwise, wrong sides facing. Open crease of fold and with wrong sides facing, bring cut edges to meet at the center fold; press. Refold along center and press, creating a double-fold bias binding. Cut binding in half to make two ties.

Attaching ties to each skirt: Cut a diagonal slash from center opening of skirt to one outside corner (through all layers). Folding raw edges of tie under, slip one binding tie over each edge of slash; pin, leaving excess length for ties at center hole; sew.

How-To's continued on page 121

MONOGRAMMED STOCKING

You need: $^2/_3$ yd red linen for stocking; $^1/_4$ yd gold silk for cuff; $^2/_3$ yd desired fabric for lining; 7" of ribbon for hanger; turquoise rayon thread (for machine embroidery) or embroidery floss (for hand embroidery) for monogram.

Cutting fabric: Enlarge pattern (page 123); add $^1/_2$" seam allowance before cutting out. Fold stocking fabric in half. Use pattern to cut two stockings from folded fabric. Repeat to cut two stocking linings. From cuff fabric, cut one $15^1/_2$" x 7" cuff.

Monogramming cuff: *You may use an embroidery sewing machine and its monogram settings/software, or you may hand embroider a monogram using a calligraphy book as a guide for lettering. Center embroidery design $3^5/_8$" from left (short) edge of cuff. Embroider monogram.*

Stitching stocking: *When sewing, place pieces right sides together and use $^1/_2$" seam.* Sew stocking pieces together, leaving top edge open. Turn.

Adding lining and hanger: *Lining* – Sew lining pieces together, leaving top edge open. Do not turn. Insert lining in stocking (wrong sides facing) with cut edges even, seams matching. *Hanger* – Fold ribbon in half. With all raw edges even, place hanger in stocking; pin hanger ends to upper back edge of lining.

Adding cuff: Press under $^1/_2$" on bottom (long) edge of cuff. Stitch short ends of cuff together, making a loop. Position cuff inside stocking with right side of cuff facing right side of lining and raw edges even. Stitch cuff to stocking. Fold cuff down over stocking.

POCKET STOCKING

You need: $^1/_2$ yd orange silk for stocking; $^1/_4$ yd red silk for cuff and pocket; $^1/_2$ yd desired fabric for lining; 1 pkg metallic gold rickrack; assorted ribbons, trims and button for embellishing.

Cutting fabric: Enlarge stocking and pocket patterns (page 124); add $^1/_2$" seam allowance to each before cutting out. Fold stocking fabric in half. Use pattern to cut two stockings from folded fabric. Repeat to cut two stocking linings. From cuff fabric, cut one $15^1/_2$" x 4" cuff and two pockets.

How-To's continued on page 121

Glorious jewel tones and rich textures aplenty combine in this magnificent array of stockings (opposite). The tree topper is actually wired-together layers of bows of graduated sizes (above).

Add some fun to the celebration by serving your guests little "gems" of wisdom. Fill empty fortune cookies with favorite sayings, printed on colored paper and cut into strips (above, left). A pyramid of freshly washed fruit makes an instant and edible accent. Choose a pedestal-style bowl so you can attach the ribbon before tying it all up in a bow (above, right).

PLAID TABLECLOTH

Size: 74" square

You need: Thai silk – 2 yds gold for center panel and binding, 1³/₄ yds plaid for borders, 13"W x 26"L each red and purple, 6¹/₂ x 13" blue and green; 4 large gold tassels.

Cutting silk: *Gold* – Cut one 44" x 44" center panel. Cut six 4"W x 44"L strips for binding. *Plaid* – Cut four identical pieces 15"W x 44"L. ***Red and purple*** – Cut two 15" x 15" squares from each. ***Blue and green*** – Cut two 7¹/₂" x 7¹/₂" squares from each.

Appliquéing small squares to gold center: Press under ¹/₄" on two adjoiningsides of each small square. With right sides of gold squares face up, pin one small square face up in each corner of gold square, raw edges even. Arrange so same colors are diagonally opposed. Topstitch squares along pressed-under edges.

Assembling: *Tablecloth is assembled in three horizontal rows of three pieces each. Pin pieces together, right sides facing; ¹/₂" seams allowed. Be sure to arrange plaid pattern (on borders) so all four pieces will be in identical positions when stitched to the gold center.* ***Row 1*** – Stitch one 15" red square and one 15" purple square to the ends of a plaid border piece. ***Row 2*** – Stitch plaid border pieces to opposite sides of the gold center panel. ***Row 3*** – Repeat

Row 1, reversing position of red and purple squares.

Binding edges: Stitch binding strips together, end to end, making one long strip. Press under both long edges ¹/₄"; press in half lengthwise. Slip binding over raw edges of cloth; pin; topstitch.

Finishing: Sew tassels to corners.

RIBBON TOPIARY

You need: Plastic foam cone; low-temp glue gun; cockscomb; 10" of 1¹/₂"W satin ribbon per "flower"; 24" of ¹/₂"W satin ribbon for ribbon topper; small ball ornaments; leaves, spray-painted gold; vase.

Making each ribbon flower: Sew a line of gathering stitches along one long edge of wide ribbon, leaving long thread ends. Pull thread ends to gather ribbon into flower shape; knot ends; cut off excess thread.

Making topiary topper: Form narrow ribbon in multi-loop bow; tie center of bow with thread.

Making topiary: Glue cone in vase. Glue cockscomb and ribbon flowers to cover cone. Glue ribbon topper to top of cone. Glue an ornament in center of each ribbon flower and topper. Glue leaves around bottom edge of cone.

Have a sweets-only party and make the dessert buffet all the more appealing with exuberant tints, from a gorgeous plaid tablecloth to a tall ribbon topiary. Hang a bay leaf and fruit garland above, and highlight it with red roses in florist's water vials.

wreaths

ENCIRCLE YOUR HOME WITH FESTIVE RINGS OF
CHRISTMAS CHEER. EMBELLISH THE SIMPLE ROUNDS
WITH ANYTHING FROM METALLIC LEAVES TO RUDDY
FRUIT. WARM FRAGRANT EUCALYPTUS IN A FAVORITE
SUNNY WINDOW. ADORN A KITCHEN WREATH WITH
COPPER MOLDS, PEPPERS AND HERBS — A DELICIOUS
SIGHT TO BEHOLD! LET YOUR GUESTS AWAKEN TO
SWEET, DRIED BLOSSOMS OR SOFT PETALS OF SILK.
THE CHOICES ARE AS ENDLESS AS YOU COULD
WISH — AND ALL ARE WITHIN YOUR REACH!

How-To's on page 126

Tidings
OF COMFORT & JOY

Whether it's the lyrics to a cherished carol or a sweetheart's **Yuletide** whispers, the magnetic pull of **prose** is undeniable. So take the words that you love from books, sheet **music**, holiday wrapping, whatever, and **transform** them into trims and decorations that cheerfully deliver your **merry** message. Write on!

A chorus of votives (above), covered in holiday paper, illuminate and captivate. A light-hearted N-O-E-L tumbles down the side of a jaunty cone (right). The delightful shape of the pinwheel star (opposite) is just as appealing now as when you were a child.

24

How-To's on page 26

Get your children to help you put together adorable decoupaged ball ornaments (above). They're a cinch to make, and the kids will be super proud when they spy them gracing your tree. A string tag garland trills across the tree (opposite), chiming out an exuberant refrain. Don the tags in ribbon and images of your choice. Make 3-D paper ornaments from the pages of old bound books. The accordion-like accents resonate with a love of reading.

PINWHEEL STAR AND ORNAMENTS

You need: Old Christmas music or color photocopies of Christmas images; spray-mount adhesive; pinking shears; glue gun; metallic red bow (optional).

Making pinwheels: Cut two 4", 6" or 9" squares of paper, depending upon desired size of pinwheel. Using spray adhesive, adhere squares with right sides out and edges even. Draw lines diagonally across square, from corner to corner. Using pinking shears, cut along each line, stopping $1/2$" from center to create four flaps. Place dot of glue in center; pull left point on one flap to center and press into glue. Place another dot of glue in center; pull left point from next flap to center in same way. Glue one point from each flap to center in same manner. For tree topper, glue bow to largest pinwheel.

CONE ORNAMENTS

You need: Tin or papier-mâché cones; color photocopies of Christmas images and alphabet; pinking shears; spray-mount adhesive; scallop-edged decorative scissors; 24" of ribbon; glue gun.

Decorating: Cut out desired images; trim edges with pinking shears. Spray backs of paper with adhesive; smooth onto cone, overlapping edges and allowing paper to extend beyond edge of cone. Glue on letters in same manner.

Finishing: Trim paper along edge of cone with scalloped scissors. Cut ribbon in half. Tie in bows. Hot glue bows to upper edge of cone.

BALL ORNAMENTS

You need: Plastic foam balls in assorted sizes; tissue paper in desired colors; foam paintbrush; decoupage medium; crafts glue; twine; pins.

Assembling: Cut tissue paper into small pieces. Brush decoupage medium onto ball; press tissue into medium to cover ball completely. Let dry; brush on additional medium and attach more tissue in overlapping layers. Apply glue in desired designs; press twine into glue and secure with pins until dry.

Finishing: Cut 6" of twine; knot ends together to form hanging loop. Coat knot with glue; pin knot to top of ball.

How-To's continued on page 127

A joyous tiding sings out from our bold appliquéd tree skirt (below). And there's no way these stockings (opposite) won't get Santa's attention. The scarf stocking is a rhapsody in red — and plaid — as it sidles up to its mock chenille counterpart made from pre-quilted muslin.

STRING TAG GARLAND

You need: 3" x 5" paper tags with strings; hole punch; photocopies of Christmas images and alphabet; pinking shears or decorative scissors; glue stick; 1/8"W ribbon in desired colors.

Assembling: Remove strings from tags. Punch hole in center bottom of each tag. Cut out motifs; trim edges with pinking shears or decorative scissors. Glue motifs and desired letters onto tag. Cut ribbon into assorted lengths. Tie tags together with ribbon at both ends to form garland.

TREE SKIRT

You need: 45"W cotton fabrics – 1 1/4 yds main color, 1/4 yd contrast color; white and matching thread; 1/4 yd paper-backed fusible web.

Cutting: From main fabric, cut 44" square. For circle, fold fabric in quarters.

Mark curved line 22" from folded corner; cut along line to form circle. Leave fabric folded. Mark curved line 3" from folded corner; cut along line to form center opening. Cut from outer edge to center opening to form back opening of skirt.

Making appliqués: Use full-size patterns (pages 132-135); trace letters onto paper side of web, leaving at least 1/2" between letters. Follow manufacturer's directions to fuse web onto wrong side of contrast fabric. Cut out letters along outlines to make appliqués. Peel off paper backing; arrange letters on right side of skirt. Following manufacturer's directions, fuse letters onto skirt. Using wide zigzag stitch and matching thread, sew around edges of each letter. Using white thread, stitch bars across letters.

Finishing: Sew zigzag stitches along all edges of skirt in same manner.

How-To's continued on page 129

Place a plethora of ribbon-wrapped goody boxes and bags in your foyer, where friends and family will be encouraged to help themselves (below). Stuff large paper cones to their tops with trinkets and trifles. Bedecked in ribbon stripes, their abundance makes for joyous season's greetings. You'll also be all set to share them with any carolers who come to call.

LARGE PAPER CONES

You need: Poster board; masking tape; foam paintbrush; decoupage medium; sheet music; color photocopies of alphabet; circle template; white paper; hole punch.

Assembling: Roll poster board into large cone; tape edges. Trim upper edge to form flat end.

Decorating: Cut sheet music into 6" squares. Brush backs of pieces with decoupage medium; smooth onto cone, overlapping edges. Let dry; apply another coat of medium if needed. Cut out alphabet; apply to cone in same manner.

Finishing: Cut 2"W strip of white paper, slightly longer than edge of cone. Fold paper accordion style; trace half of circle template along upper edge. Cut along marks to form scalloped trim. Punch holes in centers of scallops. Brush medium along straight edge of trim; press trim into position along upper edge of cone.

How-To's continued on page 129

Our jumpin' for joy pillows (above) *tell it like it is; let them serenade your guests from the corners of your sofa. They're fashioned from cozy wool, with rope letters lassoed on with fabric glue. Set up a whimsically declarative fireplace screen (left) to raise the ambience of any traditional hearthside setting.*

R(RICH RED)OSES

flowers and garlands have always set the tone for the season's celebration. This year, abandon commonplace posies and reach for not-so-expected blooms — rich, red roses. Red is for romance, revelry, rapture. Make artful arrangements that beckon with joy and imaginative color. Fill a striking garnet vase with long-stem roses and branches of rose hips. Heap a milk-glass bowl with a potpourri of fresh and dried fruit, cinnamon sticks, cloves and fragrant blossoms. Simply sublime!

REGAL FAUX LAMPS

You need: Two urns; florist foam; serrated knife; low-temp glue gun; 1" dowel; hand saw; gold spray paint; 2 clip-style lampshades; preserved or silk rose petals and greenery; sheet moss; red ribbon.

Making "lamp" base: Use knife to cut foam to fit in urns, even with tops. Glue foam in urns. Use saw to cut two pieces of dowel the desired finished height plus 3". Paint dowel pieces gold. Apply glue to one end of each dowel, then insert 3" into center of foam.

Decorating shades: Starting about 1/2" from the bottom and working in rows, glue individual rose petals around each shade. Glue greenery, small pieces at a time, along top and bottom edges of shades.

Finishing: Clip shades onto top of dowels. Glue moss over foam. Tie ribbon around each urn.

Rose petals and moss filter light through flowered shades (top), trimmed with boxwood. Place a sweet nosegay (bottom) on your door. The scent of a ravishing rosebud topiary (opposite) will make you swoon. An ivy tendril swirls a lacy touch; the base is just a plain pot covered with lush green leaves.

DOORKNOB BOUQUET HOLDER

You need: Gold wrapping paper; spray-mount adhesive; small papier-mâché cone; paper doily; wide and narrow metallic gold ribbon; glue gun; paper towels; small ornaments; tallow berries; fresh roses; florist's water vials.

Making cone: Spray back of wrapping paper with adhesive. Smooth paper around cone, trimming to fit. For hanger, cut two lengths of wide ribbon. Glue one end of each length into cone, spacing ribbons about 2" apart. Tie ribbon ends in a bow so that cone can be hung over a doorknob. Tie narrow ribbon in a bow; curl streamers. Glue ornaments, then bow to cone opposite hanger.

Assembling bouquet: Arrange doily in cone, cutting a pie-shaped wedge from doily if needed to make it fit. Place a small amount of paper towels in cone on top of doily. Trim rose stems to about 3"L; insert stems in water-filled vials. Arrange roses, bits of rose greenery and tallow berries in cone.

ROSEBUD TOPIARY

You need: Vase or desired base; large block of florist's foam; serrated knife; fresh or silk roses and ivy; garden clippers; florist's pins; assorted leaves; twisted satin cord.

Preparing base: Using knife, trim foam to fit in base so at least half of foam shows above base. Trim upper portion into slightly rounded cone shape. Remove foam.

Assembling: Clip most leaves and all thorns from rose stems; trim stems. Insert rose stems halfway into foam just above base, trimming stems if needed. Continue inserting stems into foam, starting at bottom and working toward top. Trim each row of stems slightly shorter than previous row so topiary forms cone. Arrange ivy to twist around cone, securing it in spots with florist's pins.

Finishing: Arrange leaves and cord around base. If using fresh flowers, mist daily to preserve freshness.

RUFFLED AND ROSY STOCKING

You need: Fabrics – ²/₃ yd red moiré for stocking; ²/₃ yd red cotton for lining; ¹/₄ yd gold sateen for cuff; ¹/₂ yd of 1¹/₂"W decorative ribbon; ²/₃ yd of 1¹/₂"W red velvet ribbon.

Cutting fabric: Enlarge pattern (page 137). From moiré, cut two pieces for stocking and one 2¹/₂" x 7" strip for hanging loop. From lining fabric, cut two pieces for lining front and back. From sateen, cut one 6" x 25" piece for cuff ruffle.

*B*efore Santa's visit, decorate by the chimney with care. Sumptuous materials form a quartet of petal-soft stockings.

Stitching stocking: *When sewing, place pieces right sides together and use ¹/₂" seam, unless noted.* Sew stocking pieces together, leaving top edge open. Clip seams; turn. Sew lining pieces together, leaving top edge open and an opening on one side edge. Clip seams. With right sides facing, insert stocking into lining, aligning seams. Sew top edges together. Turn through opening in lining. Slip-stitch opening closed. Push lining down into stocking.

Adding cuff: Sew short ends of cuff ruffle piece together to form a loop. Turn under one long edge ¹/₄", then ¹/₄" again; press. Topstitch to form hem. Machine-baste along remaining long edge. Pull basting thread to gather up ruffle to fit around stocking 2¹/₂" from top edge; baste ruffle to stocking. Pin decorative ribbon over raw edge of ruffle, folding raw edges of ribbon to inside. Topstitch

along top and bottom edges of ribbon.

Making rose: Roll one end of velvet ribbon into a bud shape; stitch at bottom to secure. Begin folding ribbon back over itself to form petals, tacking in place after forming each petal. Stitch end of ribbon to bottom of rose. Hand-stitch rose to stocking.

Finishing: Fold loop piece in half lengthwise; stitch long edge in ¹/₄" seam. Turn right side out; stitch close to both long edges. Fold loop in half crosswise; hand-stitch ends inside upper back corner of stocking.

VELVET STOCKING WITH RIBBON TRIMMED CUFF

You need: ²/₃ yd red velvet for stocking; ²/₃ yd red cotton for lining; ¹/₂ yd of 1¹/₂"W gold-edge velvet ribbon; ¹/₂ yd of 1"W gold metallic trim.

Cutting fabric: Enlarge pattern (page 137). From velvet, cut two pieces for stocking, one $4^{1}/_{2}$" x 15" piece for cuff and one $2^{1}/_{2}$" x 7" strip for hanging loop. From lining fabric, cut two pieces for lining front and back. From ribbon and trim, cut one 15" piece each.

Stitching stocking: *When sewing, place pieces right sides together and use $^{1}/_{2}$" seam, unless noted.* Sew stocking pieces together, leaving top edge open. Clip seams; turn. Sew lining pieces together, leaving top edge open. Clip seams. With wrong sides facing, insert lining into stocking, aligning seams.

Making cuff: Press under $^{1}/_{2}$" on one long edge of cuff (bottom). Place ribbon on right side of cuff, aligning bottom edges. "Sandwich" straight edge of metallic trim between ribbon and cuff. Topstitch along bottom and top edges of ribbon to secure. Fold cuff in half, right sides together, matching short edges. Sew short edges together to form a loop. Turn.

Making hanging loop: Fold loop strip in half lengthwise; stitch long edge in $^{1}/_{4}$" seam. Turn right side out; stitch close to both long edges. Fold loop in half crosswise; pin inside stocking lining at back edge, aligning raw edges of loop and lining.

Assembling: Insert cuff into lining with right sides facing and matching raw edges. Sew cuff and stocking together. Pull cuff out of stocking and fold down.

WOVEN RIBBONS STOCKING

You need: $^{2}/_{3}$ yd red cotton fabric for stocking; $^{2}/_{3}$ yd red lining fabric; $^{2}/_{3}$ yd paper-backed fusible web; assorted red and metallic gold ribbons and trims; 2 yds metallic gold piping.

Making lattice fabric: Cut a 13" x 20" piece from stocking fabric. Fuse web to right side of fabric piece; remove backing. Arrange ribbons and trims diagonally across fabric, so that long edges are touching; pin. Weave additional ribbons and trims from the opposite direction to create a lattice effect; pin. Fuse ribbons and trims in place.

Cutting pieces: Enlarge pattern (page 137). From lattice fabric, cut stocking front. From remaining cotton, cut stocking back and one $2^{1}/_{2}$" x 7" strip for hanging loop. From lining fabric, cut two pieces for lining front and back.

Stitching stocking: *When sewing, place pieces right sides together and use $^{1}/_{2}$" seam, unless noted.* Matching raw edges, baste piping to sides and bottom of stocking front. Sew stocking pieces together, leaving top edge open. Clip seams; turn. Baste piping to top edge of stocking.

Adding lining: Sew lining pieces together, leaving top edge open and an opening on one side edge. Clip seams.

Making hanging loop: Fold loop strip in half lengthwise; stitch long edge in $^{1}/_{4}$" seam. Turn right side out; stitch close to both long edges. Fold loop in half crosswise; pin inside stocking lining at back edge, aligning raw edges of loop and lining.

For a beautiful kissing ball that never fades (top), poke faux flowers and mistletoe into a foam ball and hot-glue on a ribbon hanger. Make an everyday chair sing with a French-horn ornament, ribbons and fresh roses (bottom).

How-To's continued on page 136

GLORIOUS
garlands

DECK THE HALLS, THE HEARTH — THE WHOLE

HOUSE — WITH BOUGHS OF JOY. DRAPE THE BANISTER

WITH A MÉLANGE OF GREEN-AND-GOLD, OR LOOP

SWAGS OF PINE INTO CHEERY WREATHS. REFLECT THE

RADIANCE OF CHRISTMAS WITH SPRAYS OF METALLIC

LEAVES, SILVER BALLS AND FROSTED FLORA. MAKE

YOUR MANTEL MAGICAL WITH A WINTRY ARRAY OF

SNOWY VINES AND FRUIT, OR LET SWEET NOSTALGIA

WARM THE FIRESIDE WITH GREETING CARDS

AND EVERLASTINGS. FA-LA-LA-LA-LA!

jazzy and bRiGhT

Who says Christmas has to be red and green? Certainly not us. For the designs presented on these pages, we found our inspiration in the electric shades of Miami in the 50's, the retro chic of the Floridian seaside. The results were surprisingly modern and refreshingly fun.

How-To's on page 138

JEWELED ORNAMENTS

You need: Glass ball ornaments in assorted sizes; glue gun; imitation flat-back gemstones and beads; dimensional paint writers in assorted colors.

Assembling: Glue larger gems onto ornaments. Apply dots of paint as desired; press smaller gems and beads into paint. Let dry. Paint desired designs on ornaments; let dry.

FOLDED RIBBON STAR

You need (for each 4$\frac{1}{2}$" star): 3 yds of $\frac{1}{2}$"W or $\frac{5}{8}$"W ribbon; thick craft glue; fine cord.

Assembling base: Cut four 27" pieces of ribbon. Fold each piece in half crosswise; trim ends diagonally. Place one piece vertically, ends pointed up. Place second piece to right of first piece, ends pointed down; strips should be aligned for about 2" near folds. Slip fold of first piece between layers of a third piece, placing this third piece horizontally. Hold ends of third piece together and pull them between layers of second piece, weaving them together. Slip fold of second piece between layers of a fourth piece, placing this fourth piece horizontally. Hold ends together and pull between layers of first strip in same manner. Pull each strip outward to form square woven base.

Forming first layer: Fold top layer of left vertical piece down over other pieces; press to crease. Rotate work one-quarter turn clockwise. Fold top layer down and press in same manner. Rotate and crease next piece in same manner. Insert fourth piece between layers of lower left square formed by these folds; pull end of piece down. Crease and rotate in same manner.

Forming star points: Fold upper right strip down at a 45-degree angle, so it is horizontal. Fold it down again at a 45-degree angle, so it is vertical again; press to crease, forming a point (inverted "V"). Fold this point in half down its center, forming a triangle. Insert end of this piece between layers of upper right square, forming star point. Rotate work one-quarter turn clockwise. Repeat folding and creasing three more times to make four star points in this manner.

Making back of star: Turn star over. Make four star points same as for front of star.

Making upper points on both sides: Lift upper right horizontal piece to the left so lower right vertical piece can be folded up. Press to crease. Fold this piece over itself at 45-degree angle; crease. Hold end of piece, keeping this side of piece facing up as you turn piece counter-clockwise; insert end between layers of upper left square. Pull end of strip out through star point; use fingers to open out point, if needed. Pull tight to make upward-pointing star point. Rotate star. Make next three star points in same manner, rotating after each. Turn star over to make upward-pointing star points on back of star.

Finishing: Trim ribbon ends even with edges of outer star points. Glue ends in place to secure; let dry. Stitch cord through one point of star to make hanger; knot ends together.

LOOPED GARLAND

You need: 1"W single-face satin ribbons – 1 roll of each of lime green, hot pink, turquoise, orange; pinking shears; glue gun.

Assembling: Cut ribbon into 10" or 7" pieces, depending on desired width of garland. To make first ring, overlap ends of ribbon 1" and glue. Slip another color of ribbon through ring; glue ends in same manner. Continue adding rings in same manner until garland is as desired.

How-To's continued on page 138

Shake it up! Put an original twist on the traditional this season: A jeweled ornament, resplendent ribbon star and looped garland (opposite) proudly pizzazz a snowy white tree. Go for the glow on a mantel with an imaginatively swooped garland and a funky finial accent (this page, top). Place bonny beaded baubles in a colorful bowl (bottom) for an unexpected centerpiece.

HOLIDAY STOCKINGS

You need: Silk shantung fabrics – $^1/_2$ yd each main fabric (or use organza for main fabric), lining and piping; $^1/_2$ yd fusible fleece; 2 yds cotton cording.

Cutting: Enlarge pattern (page 139). Fuse fleece onto wrong side of main fabric. From main fabric, cut two pieces for stocking front and back and one $2^1/_2$" x 7" strip for hanging loop. From lining fabric, cut two pieces for lining front and back. From piping fabric, cut $2^1/_2$"W bias strips; piece strips together to form bias strip about 2 yds long.

Making piping: *When sewing, place pieces right sides together and use $^1/_2$" seam, unless otherwise noted.* Fold bias strip in half lengthwise, right side out. Place cording in fold; stitch close to base of cording to make piping. Baste piping to sides and lower edges of stocking front, placing piping stitching $^1/_2$" from edges. Place front and back together, with right sides facing and raw edges even. Stitch sides and lower edges, leaving upper edge open. Stitch lining sections together (without piping) in same manner, also leaving a 4" opening along back edge. Baste piping to upper edge of stocking. Place stocking in lining with right sides facing and seams aligned. Stitch lining to stocking along upper edge. Turn stocking through opening in lining. Push lining down into stocking.

Finishing: Fold loop in half lengthwise; stitch long edge in $^1/_4$" seam. Turn right side out; stitch close to both long edges. Fold loop in half crosswise; hand-stitch ends inside upper back corner of stocking.

Go ahead and hang the stockings with care, but craft them out of sensuous silk shantung with piping and diaphanous organza. Their flair undeniable, these swank holiday socks are in a class by themselves.

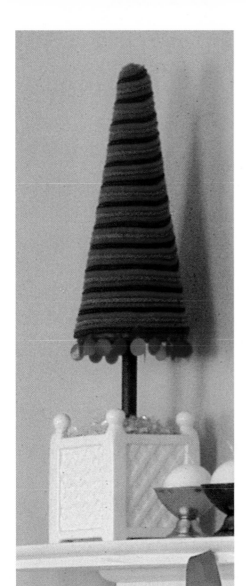

BRAIDED TOPIARIES

You need: 13" high plastic foam cone; 1/2 yd sequin fringe trim; glue gun; braided rope trim – 3 1/2 yds each of 4 colors; 15"L piece of 3/4" dowel; paintbrush; acrylic paint in desired color; old mixing bowl; plaster of paris; terra-cotta pot without drainage hole; masking tape.

Decorating cone: Glue fringe trim to lower edge of cone. Place small amount of glue at base of cone. Place ends of all 4 braids in glue. Wrap braids around cone, gluing as you wrap and keeping braids aligned but not overlapping. At top, apply glue and form spiral with braid ends. Trim excess.

Assembling topiary: Paint dowel; let dry. Following manufacturer's directions, mix plaster in bowl. Pour into pot; allow to set for several minutes, then stand dowel in center. Place strips of tape across top of pot to brace dowel in position. Allow to dry overnight. Using scissors, make a small hole in center of cone base; place small amount of glue in hole. Place cone on dowel; let dry.

GIFT PACKAGE PLACE MATS

You need (for 4 place mats): Silk shantung fabrics – 1/2 yd green, 1/4 yd blue, 1/4 yd fuchsia, 5/8 yd plaid; 7/8 yd backing fabric; low-loft quilt batting; monofilament nylon thread.

Cutting: Cutting on crosswise grain across full width of fabric, cut the following pieces – two 6 1/2" strips from green for fronts, two 2" strips from blue for sides, four 2" strips from fuchsia for tops. Cut the following pieces from plaid in same manner – four 1 1/2" strips and one 1 1/4" strip for ribbon. Also cut the following from plaid – eight 6 1/2" squares for bows and one 2 1/2 x 15" strip for bow loops. From backing, cut four 13 1/2" x 17 1/2" rectangles; cut four matching pieces from batting.

Making fronts: *All stitching is done in 1/4" seams, with right sides facing and raw edges even, unless noted.* Stitch front strips to each side of a 1 1/2" ribbon strip to make package fronts; press seams toward ribbon. From this piece, cut four 9 1/2" x 13 1/2" rectangles for fronts.

How-To's continued on page 138

R*ules — especially when it comes to interior decorating — are made to be broken. Gift package place mats and lightbulb place cards (bottom) will set your table with style and humor. A braided topiary (top, left), edged in sparkling sequins, makes a spirited mantel sentry. Tie a festive bow in an unusual spot (top, right) for a little extra jazz.*

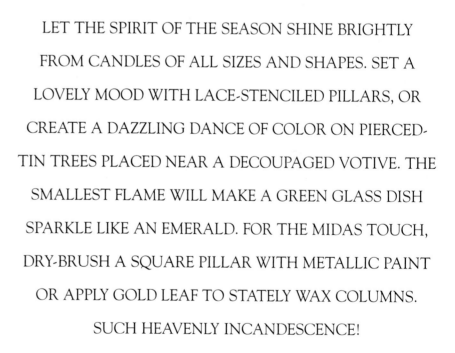

candles
ALL AGLOW

LET THE SPIRIT OF THE SEASON SHINE BRIGHTLY
FROM CANDLES OF ALL SIZES AND SHAPES. SET A
LOVELY MOOD WITH LACE-STENCILED PILLARS, OR
CREATE A DAZZLING DANCE OF COLOR ON PIERCED-
TIN TREES PLACED NEAR A DECOUPAGED VOTIVE. THE
SMALLEST FLAME WILL MAKE A GREEN GLASS DISH
SPARKLE LIKE AN EMERALD. FOR THE MIDAS TOUCH,
DRY-BRUSH A SQUARE PILLAR WITH METALLIC PAINT
OR APPLY GOLD LEAF TO STATELY WAX COLUMNS.
SUCH HEAVENLY INCANDESCENCE!

How-To's on page 140

DECOUPAGED MITTEN BOX

You need: Mitten-shaped papier-mâché box; gift wrap in assorted designs; foam paintbrush; decoupage medium; dimensional paint markers.

Decorating: Cut gift wrap into assorted rectangles. Brush decoupage medium onto back of each; press onto box and lid, smoothing from center out to remove air bubbles. Cover entire box and lid in same way; let dry. Brush with additional coat of decoupage medium; let dry. Using paint markers, draw ¼" "stitches" along edges of paper rectangles; let dry.

HEART ORNAMENTS

You need: Fabric scraps in assorted red and green prints; assorted ribbons, buttons and other trims; fiberfill stuffing.

Cutting: Enlarge pattern (page 142). For each ornament, cut two hearts from coordinating fabrics for ornament front and back.

Sewing: *All stitching is done in ¼" seams, with right sides facing and raw edges even, unless noted.* Pin ribbon to outer edge of one heart, if desired; baste ¼" from edge. Or, pin lengths of ribbon across one heart; stitch close to both edges. Cut 6" of ribbon for hanging loop; fold in half. Pin raw ends to right side of one heart at center top. Stitch heart front to back, leaving opening along one side. Trim seams and clip curves; turn. Stuff firmly; slip-stitch opening closed. Sew buttons randomly to front.

How-To's continued on page 51

cozy country CHARM

decorate your home with patchwork and plaid for the **coziest** Christmas ever. All through the house, it's the personal touches that stir the soul. For instance, bring an old-fashioned feel to any room with these fun and easy-to-make **trims** and ornaments that reflect the simple charm of a **country** Christmas. Have a homespun holiday with a handmade look!

Trim the tree with a mix of store-bought and your own ribbon and heart ornaments (opposite and page 50). To remind Santa how good you've been, tuck cookies into a merry decoupaged mitten box (above).

Make the season super bright with colorful ribbon and heart ornaments. The balls are covered with red and green ribbons, the hearts fashioned from fabric remnants. All are embellished with buttons, bows and other flourishes. And oh, what fun it is to find piles of prettily wrapped presents stacked on a red and white patchwork tree skirt (opposite).

RIBBON BALL ORNAMENTS

You need: Plastic foam balls in varied sizes; plaid and solid ribbons in assorted colors and widths; glue gun; pins; silk holly or pine sprigs.

Decorating: Cut wider ribbons into short pieces; wrap and glue around each ball. Glue narrow solid ribbon around ball, covering seams of other ribbons. Cut 6" of narrow ribbon; fold in half and push a pin through ends to form hanging loop. Coat tip of pin with glue; push into top of ball. Pin holly or pine sprig at base of loop, if desired.

PATCHWORK TREE SKIRT

You need: $1/2$ yd each of 5 different red plaid and striped fabrics; air-soluble fabric marker.

Cutting: From one striped fabric, cut a $1^1/2$"W bias strip at least $4^1/2$ yds long (pieced as needed) for outer binding. From another fabric, cut a $2^1/2$" x $26^1/2$" facing strip. Cut remaining fabrics into $4^1/2$" squares and $4^1/2$" x $6^1/2$" rectangles for patchwork.

Making patchwork: *All stitching is done in $1/4$" seams, with right sides facing and raw edges even, unless noted.* Pin and stitch patchwork pieces together along $4^1/2$" sides, forming 12 strips, each at least 50" long. Pin and stitch strips together along long edges forming patchwork at least 50" square.

Making skirt: Fold patchwork square in quarters. Mark a curved line 25" from corner; cut along this line to form 50" circle. On right side, mark straight line from center to edge along straight grain. Press under $1/4$" on one short end and both long edges of facing strip. Pin strip to skirt, aligning and basting along marked lines. Stitch "U"-shaped line, $1/4$" on each side of marked line. Slash along marked line; turn facing to wrong side of skirt. Stitch along outer pressed edges through all layers.

Finishing: Fold under $1/4$" on long edges of binding; press. Fold binding in half, right sides out; press. Pin binding over outer edge of skirt, encasing raw edges; stitch close to folds.

PATCHWORK STOCKING

You need: 5 coordinated dish towels; tracing paper; 2 skeins of red embroidery floss.

Cutting: Enlarge pattern (page 141). Trace stocking outline and each A, B, C, D and E area separately; add $1/2$" all around each piece. Use stocking outline pattern to cut one back from a towel. Use remaining patterns to cut one each of front patches from assorted towels.

Assembling front: *All stitching is done in $1/2$" seams, with right sides facing and raw edges even, unless noted.* Stitch patches together, trimming each seam after stitching; front should be same size as back.

Making stocking: Stitch front to back, leaving upper edge open. Clip curves; turn. Turn under $1/2$" on upper edge; stitch close to fold to hem stocking.

Finishing: Using two strands of floss, sew blanket stitches around all edges of stocking. Cut 3" x 8" piece from a towel scrap for hanging loop. Turn under $1/4$" on each raw edge; press. Fold in half lengthwise, right side out; press. Stitch close to fold. Fold loop in half; stitch to upper back edge of stocking.

LADYBUG STOCKING

You need: Dish towels – 2 green waffle-weave, 1 red ladybug print with woven edges.

Cutting patterns: Enlarge pattern (page 141). Trace once; add $1/2$" all around for stocking front and back. Trace heel and toe patches along dashed lines; add $1/2$" all around to make patterns for patches.

Cutting fabric pieces: From green towels, cut one front and one back. From ladybug towel, cut one heel and one toe, centering motifs; also cut one 8" x 23" cuff, placing hemmed edge of towel on long edge of cuff.

Assembling front: Press under $1/2$" on inner edges of patches; pin to stocking front, right sides up. Stitch close to pressed edges; baste close to outer edges.

Making stocking: *All stitching is done in $1/2$" seams, with right sides facing and raw*

Rock the rafters with one-of-a-kind stockings (above). There'll be no mistaking whose is whose when it comes time to fill them to the top with gads of gifts. Not even Scrooge could resist these beguiling birdhouses (opposite). Don them in gay apparel: feathery wisps of evergreen, beaded necklaces of holly and satiny toppers of ribbon, then nestle them onto a bookshelf or bench.

How-To's continued on page 54

edges even, *unless noted.* Stitch front to back, leaving upper edge open. Clip curves; turn. Fold cuff in half crosswise; stitch short ends together to form tube. Place cuff inside stocking, with right side of cuff aligned with wrong side of stocking; stitch upper edge. Fold cuff to right side so towel hem forms lower edge. **Finishing**: Cut 3" x 8" piece of green towel for hanging loop. Turn under $1/4$" on each raw edge; press. Fold in half lengthwise, right side out; press. Stitch close to fold. Fold loop in half; stitch to upper back edge of stocking.

SOCK STOCKING

You need: Tweed sweat sock; 48 assorted buttons; $3/4$ yd of $1 1/2$"W ribbon; small amount of raffia.
Decorating: Turn down small cuff on stocking. Sew buttons to stocking as desired. Tie ribbon in bow; stitch to cuff. Form small loop from raffia; stitch inside back of cuff for hanging loop.

HOLLY STOCKING

You need: Felt – $1/2$ yd white, 9" x 12" piece each of 3 shades of green; embroidery floss – green, red; twenty-two $7/16$" red wooden beads; $1 1/2$ yds of $1 1/2$"W red velvet ribbon.
Cutting: Enlarge patterns (page 141). From white felt, cut stocking front and back. From each shade of green, cut 20 leaves.
Making stocking: Pin stocking front to back, with raw edges even. Stitch in $1/4$" seams, leaving upper edge open. Clip curves; turn.
Appliquéing leaves: Pin overlapping leaves to stocking front; keep hand inside stocking to prevent pinning through back of stocking. Using green floss, sew running stitches down center of each leaf. Using red floss, sew bead berries as desired.
Finishing: Cut 8" length of ribbon. Fold in half; stitch ribbon ends to back edge of stocking for hanging loop. Tie remaining ribbon in bow; trim each end in a "V". Stitch bow to hanging loop.

CHAIR-BACK HEART

You need: Fabric scraps in assorted red and green prints; assorted rickrack, ribbons, buttons and other trims; fiberfill stuffing.
Making patchwork: *All stitching is done in $1/4$" seams, with right sides facing and raw edges even, unless noted.* Cut fabric scraps into straight-sided shapes. Stitch pairs of shapes together; press seams open. Continue to pin and stitch pieces together to form patchwork at least 11" x 22". Stitch rickrack and ribbon over seams.
Assembling: Enlarge pattern (page 142). Cut two large hearts from patchwork for front and back. Stitch front to back, leaving opening along one side. Trim seams and clip curves; turn. Stuff firmly; slip-stitch opening closed. Sew buttons randomly to front. Cut two 10" pieces of ribbon; stitch center of each to tops of heart for ties.

FESTIVE SHELF EDGING

You need: Gift wrap on rolls – red, white; transfer paper; crafts knife; cutting mat; scalloped-edge decorative scissors.
To do: Enlarge pattern (page 145). For edging, cut a piece of red gift wrap 8"W and desired length. Beginning at one short edge, fold paper at 18" intervals, accordion-style. Align edges of pattern to edges of folded paper. Use transfer paper to transfer pattern onto top layer of folded paper. Place paper on cutting mat; use crafts knife to cut out through all layers. Use scissors to cut along edges. For edging liner, cut out a scalloped length of white gift wrap in same manner, omitting lacy design.

How-To's continued on page 140

*B*ring joy to any room with our easy snowman garland (top). *Simply tie a lacy snowflake decoration to a holiday garland with ribbon, then loop it to hold back a curtain. Our dear chair-back heart (bottom) is made like the heart ornaments, but you add ribbon ties for hanging.*

Clip red edging into a pretty pattern, then back it with white paper (left) to dress up plain shelving. Add a bouquet of pinecones, wired onto florist's picks, and a plateful of pomanders for holiday fragrance. Add to the Yuletide spirit with some poinsettia pillows (below). The dreamy designs are felt-on-felt appliqué.

IT'S A
wrap!

WRAP, STACK AND ROLL UP THE
GIFTS! COAX FLOWING FABRICS AND
PRETTY PAPERS AROUND CURVED
PARCELS, TWIST THEM AT ENDS AND
FOLD THEM AT CORNERS. SLIDE
SPECIAL CHRISTMAS TOKENS INTO
BEAUTIFUL BAGS YOU'VE STITCHED.
THEN BIND EVERYTHING WITH
BUNCHES OF RAFFIA OR ELEGANT
TANGLES OF RIBBON AND CORD. MAKE
ALL YOUR HOLIDAY PRESENTATIONS
INTO RAZZLE-DAZZLE DELIGHTS!

How-To's on page 146

Merry Christmas and a Happy New Year!

Compliments of SANTA CLAUS

How-To's on page 147

perfect presents

Iend Santa a helping hand with these **great** gifts. What better way to show how much you **care** than by making friends and family something exactly right for them? Whether it's a **doll** for Darla, a velvet muffler for Grandpa or frames for your next-door neighbor … whoever it's for, it's made by **you**!

A *wondrous box of wooden blocks* (opposite) *is destined to become an heirloom. Sit down at this pretty desk set* (top) *to address holiday cards. A velvet muffler* (middle) *is just the thing for that special someone. Or create richly trimmed pillows from bright silk* (bottom).

A YEAR OF FRAMES

You need: 12 paperboard frames; acrylic paint; paintbrushes; transfer type; glue gun; metal or wood cutouts; ribbons; glitter; seasonal trims (e.g., snowflakes for December, skates for January; hearts for February, etc.).

To do: Paint frame as desired; let dry. Label month with transfer type. Decorate frame as you wish with trims and various seasonal motifs.

FABRIC-COVERED JOURNALS

You need: Journal(s); sheer metallic fabric; photocopy of photo/greeting card; jewel glue; $1/2$"W metallic ribbon; ball or beads.

Measuring, cutting fabric: Measure enough sheer fabric to create a sleeve to fit over front and back covers, inside and out, $3/8$" allowed all around for seams at top and bottom and small hem on short sides. Cut fabric.

Appliquéing photo: Wrap fabric around journal, positioned as it will be in finished sleeve. Cut small piece of fabric $1/2$" larger than photo. Layer photo, then small piece of fabric on front cover. Stitch through fabric and photo, about $1/8$" in from outer edges of photo. Tack or glue beads along lines of stitches.

Stitching sleeve: Hem short sides of sleeve. With right sides facing, fold short ends in toward center, leaving a middle space open for at least the width of book spine. Stitch seams along top/bottom of sleeve; turn. Slip cover on journal.

Making bookmark: Cut ribbon to length of journal plus a few inches. Glue ball on end or slip beads on end and knot. Sew other end inside top middle edge of sleeve.

How-To's continued on page 147

BOTTLE STOPPERS

You need: Wooden beads (5 to 6 per stopper); clear-drying multipurpose cement; brushes; acrylic paints; flat-back rhinestones; cork; gift glass bottle(s) (optional).

To do (for each): Paint beads as desired. Stack and glue beads together to form pattern desired. Glue on rhinestones. Glue cork to bottom bead. Insert cork in bottle (optional).

Fashion a year's worth of picture frames, each suggesting a different month (opposite, top). For diary keepers, create elegant fabric-covered journals (opposite, bottom). Set trinkets inside soaps for a charming offering full of surprises (left). Be as fanciful as you like combining jewels and painted wooden shapes into towering bottle stoppers (below).

SWEATER MITTENS

You need: Old sweaters made from 100-percent unwashable wool (to insure shrinkage when washed); chalk pencil.

Preparing wool: Machine-wash sweaters in hot water; machine- or line-dry to make thick wool fabric.

Cutting: Enlarge pattern (page 148). For each pair of mittens, cut two hands, two thumbs and two cuffs from washed wool. Transfer markings to wool.

Sewing: *All stitching is done in ¹/₄" seams, with right sides facing and raw edges even, unless noted.* Pin thumb to hand along marked straight edges, matching marks. Stitch from circle to lower edge on each side. Fold hand and thumb so seams are aligned and raw edges are even. Stitch from hand fold to thumb fold. Clip seam allowance at circles. Fold cuff in half crosswise, aligning marks; stitch marked end, forming tube. Fold cuff in half, right side out. Place cuff inside mitten, right sides facing, aligning cuff seam with mark on lower edge of mitten. Stitch cuff to mitten. Turn right side out.

MISS HOLLY DOLL

You need: Fabrics – $^3/_4$ yd unbleached muslin, $^1/_2$ yd yellow fleece (fluffy on both sides), $^1/_2$ yd red corduroy, $^1/_4$ yd red lining fabric, $^1/_4$ yd blue cotton; remnant of green felt; $^1/_2$ yd of 1"W green gingham ribbon; 4" square of paper-backed fusible web; fiberfill stuffing; brown or red carpet yarn; embroidery floss – white, brown; fabric glue; 2 small yellow buttons; cosmetic blush; medium-weight cardboard.

Cutting: Enlarge patterns (pages 150-152). From muslin, cut one head front, one upper head back, one lower head back, four ear sections, one nose, two body sections and four arm sections. From fleece, cut one shirt front, two shirt backs and two shirt cuffs. From corduroy, cut two overall sections, one pocket and two straps. From lining fabric, cut two overall linings, one pocket lining and two strap lining sections. From blue cotton, cut four leg sections. Trace tree onto paper side of web. Fuse web onto wrong side of green felt. Cut out along outline.

Embroidering face: Using brown floss, stitch eyes and mouth. Using white floss, stitch highlight on each eye.

Making body: *All stitching is done in $^1/_4$" seams, with right sides facing and raw edges even, unless noted.* **Head** – Stitch head back sections together, leaving 2" opening in center. Stitch head front to back. Clip curves; turn. Stuff firmly; slip-stitch opening closed. Stitch each pair of ears together, leaving straight edge open. Clip curves; turn. Stuff lightly. Turn under $^1/_4$" on open edge; slip-stitch ears to sides of head. Sew hand gathering stitches close to edge of nose; place small amount of stuffing in center, then pull up threads. Make several small stitches to secure. Glue nose to center of face. **Body** – Stitch front to back, leaving open on lower edge and where marked on sides.

How-To's continued on page 149

Surprise: These wooly sweater mittens (opposite) are nifty no-knits! Just snip and sew to recycle pullovers and cardigans into cozy covers. And our cuddlesome Miss Holly doll invites lots of affection with her cozy red corduroys, comfy fleece sweater and sunny smile. Mr. Clown, with his perky polka-dot ruff, is equally appealing as he snuggles next to Mr. Bear in the gaily striped stocking.

CHEERY STATIONERY

You need: Blank cards and envelopes; acrylic paints; wooden star ornament; foam brush; paper twist.

To do: Paint vertical, then horizontal stripes on fronts of note cards and backs of envelopes; let dry. Paint ornament. Tie cards and envelopes together with paper twist. Attach ornament to bow.

DOGGIE FRAME

You need: Flat wooden frame; dog biscuits; glue gun; spray sealer.

To do: Remove backing and glass from frame. Glue dog biscuits to frame. Spray with sealer. Reassemble frame.

ETCHED VASES

You need: Assorted glass vases; holiday stencils; etching cream; stencil adhesive; lint-free cloths; glass cleaner; soft paintbrush.

To do: Wash and dry vases with glass cleaner and cloths. Spray back of stencil with adhesive; position on vase as desired. Follow etching cream manufacturer's directions to apply etching cream over stencils. Allow cream to set; wash thoroughly. Remove stencils; wash again.

NAPPING MAT AND PILLOW

You need: Fleece fabric – 2 yds each yellow, red; 8" x 12" piece of black felt; five 8" x 12" pieces of calico fabric; 1 yd paper-backed fusible web; 1³/₄ yds of 1"W black ribbon; air-soluble fabric marker; fiberfill stuffing.

Cutting: Enlarge patterns (page 153). Trace head pattern five times, ear pattern 10 times and body pattern five times onto paper side of fusible web, leaving ¹/₂" between pieces; cut out pieces. Fuse heads and ears onto felt and each body onto calico; cut out along outlines. From yellow fleece, cut 24" x 42" mat front, 6" x 42" bag strap and 12" x 16" pillow front. From red fleece, cut 26" x 44" mat back, 18" x 42" bag and 14" x 18" pillow back. Fuse web onto ribbon. Cut twenty 3" pieces of ribbon for legs; cut one end of each leg in a "V".

Embroidering: Write a number from 1 to 5 on each sheep body. Using red thread and wide machine zigzag stitch, embroider numbers (stitch through web backing paper).

Making mat: Peel paper backing off sheep 1 through 4 and 16 legs. Arrange four sheep bodies on mat front; fuse. Arrange heads, ears and legs around body; fuse. Sew wide machine zigzag stitches around each sheep. Center and pin mat front on mat back, right sides up; stitch ¹/₄" from edges of front.

Making bag: Turn under ¹/₂" on one short end of bag; stitch close to fold to hem bag. Fold bag in half crosswise, with right sides facing and short raw edge extending 3" past hemmed edge; pin sides. Stitch sides in ¹/₄" seams. Fold strap in half lengthwise; stitch close to all edges. Stitch ends of strap inside bag. Turn bag right side out; center, then stitch raw edge of bag to top edge of mat. For carrying, fold up mat and tuck into bag.

Making pillow: Fuse remaining sheep on pillow front in same way as for mat front. Center and pin pillow front on pillow back, right sides up; stitch ¹/₄" from edges of front, leaving opening on one side. Stuff; slip-stitch opening closed.

MR. CLAUS BOXES

You need: 5 hexagonal papier-mâché boxes in graduated sizes; wood pieces – one 2³/₈" disc, two 1¹/₂" discs, 1 large ruffled heart, two 1³/₄" ruffled hearts, one 1" ball knob; 1 pair doll glasses; 2 small wiggle eyes; ¹/₂ yd muslin; 10" of thin wire; velvet Santa hat; paintbrushes – sponge, flat, liner; acrylic paints – flesh, light red, dark red, black, white, silver; crafts glue; snow texture paint; satin-finish spray varnish; crafts stick; sandpaper; awl; tissue paper.

Assembling: *Boxes are numbered from smallest to largest.* Paint box and lid 3, box 4 and box and lid 5 light red; let dry.

Using sponge bush, apply light coat of dark red over light red basecoat. Paint lid 4 and large disc black; let dry. Paint edge of black disc and all hearts silver; let dry. Paint box 2, small discs and ball knob with flesh; let dry. Fill hat with tissue paper. Place lid on box 1; place hat over box, pulling hat rim over lid 2. Glue hat to lid 2. Using black paint, write "Ho! Ho! Ho!" on large heart; glue onto hat. Apply light strokes of light red to small discs and ball to make cheeks and nose. Paint highlights on cheeks and nose with white; let dry. Glue cheeks and nose on box 2. Punch holes in sides of box. Place glasses on face. To make beard, tear muslin into ½" strips; cut

twenty-nine 12" lengths. Fold in half; knot onto wire. Insert wire ends through glasses, then through holes in box; twist ends together inside box. Tear small muslin strips; glue under hat rim. Trim beard as desired. To make fur, use crafts stick to apply one coat of snow texture paint; let dry, then apply another coat. Apply 2" band of fur around lower edge of box 5. Place box 4 on box 5; apply 2" band of fur up center of both boxes. While fur is wet, press small hearts in place. Glue remaining disc at neck edge. **Finishing:** Coat boxes 3, 4 and 5 with varnish; let dry. Stack boxes.

How-To's continued on page 150

Cheery stationery (opposite, left) starts with plain cards and envelopes. You just paint on the patterns and rope together with a rustic raffia bow. Perfect for a pet-loving pal, a fetching doggie frame (opposite, middle) will be treasured for years to come. Hot-glue real dog biscuits to a purchased frame and insert Fido's photo. Lickety-split, you're done! For etched vases (opposite, right), cascade a spray of stars down the side or transfer holly leaves onto a plain glass container. You can count on sweet dreams for a toddler with our baa-baa black sheep napping mat and pillow (this page, left), created from fleece, of course. And Mr. and Mrs. Claus (below) will stack up to be a couple's favorite gift this year. You can even tuck a few trinkets inside the tiers.

Tree-shaped and decorated with candy stars, Apricot Holiday Bread (below) makes a thoughtful gift for a busy family. Divide a batch of quick-&-easy Peanut Sesame Brittle (opposite) into jars to please all the nut-lovers in your life.

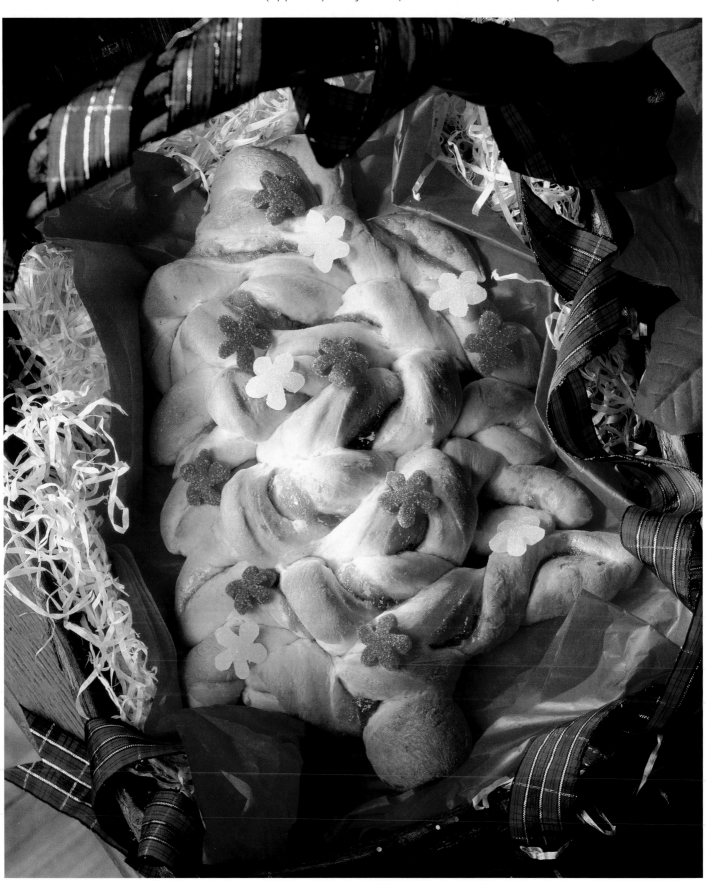

incredible edibles
GIFTS FROM THE KITCHEN

Whether you have a neighbor with a sweet tooth or a co-worker with a taste for savory treats, you're sure to find the perfect present among these goodies to give. And *voila!* These sensational snacks and flavorful condiments are mostly make-ahead.

APRICOT HOLIDAY BREAD

- ³/₄ cup water
- ³/₄ cup milk
- ¹/₄ cup (¹/₂ stick) unsalted butter
- 4¹/₂ to 4³/₄ cups all-purpose flour
- ¹/₂ cup sugar
- 1 tablespoon grated lemon zest
- ³/₄ teaspoon salt
- ¹/₄ teaspoon ground allspice
- 1 package (¹/₄ ounce) quick-rising yeast

Apricot Filling:
- ¹/₂ cup quartered dried apricot halves
- ¹/₂ cup firmly packed light-brown sugar
- ¹/₂ cup unsweetened applesauce
- ³/₄ teaspoon ground ginger
  Star-shaped candies, for garnish (optional)

1. Combine water, milk and butter in small saucepan. Heat over low heat until very warm (125° to 130° on instant-read thermometer).
2. Combine 2 cups flour, sugar, lemon zest, salt, allspice and yeast in large bowl. Add heated milk mixture. Beat on medium speed for 3 minutes. Stir in 2¹/₄ cups of flour to make a soft dough.
3. Turn dough out onto a lightly floured surface. Knead 20 times, adding more flour as needed to prevent sticking. Place dough in large greased bowl, turning to coat. Cover and let rise in warm place until doubled, about 30 minutes.
4. Meanwhile, prepare Apricot Filling: Combine dried apricots, brown sugar, applesauce and ginger in small saucepan.

Bring to a simmer; cook 12 to 15 minutes or until thickened. Pour into food processor. Whirl until smooth purée.
5. Coat large baking sheet with nonstick vegetable-oil cooking spray.
6. Punch down dough. Transfer to lightly floured surface. Pat the dough out into a 14 x 12-inch triangle. Mark center by pressing a vertical indent in dough from top point to bottom center of base.
7. Spread cooled Apricot Filling over one half of triangle, leaving a ³/₄-inch border along 2 exterior sides. Fold other half over on top; press edges together to seal. Transfer to prepared baking sheet.
8. Starting at the diagonal side opposite the folded side, with kitchen scissors, cut parallel lines through dough, perpendicular to the folded edge and at 1-inch intervals, to within ³/₄ inch of folded side. Alternating strips, fold strips

to opposite side. Twist strips to make tree shape. Shape bottom strip to form base.
9. Cover and let rise 45 minutes or until almost doubled.
10. Heat oven to 350°.
11. Bake bread in 350° oven for 25 minutes or until golden brown and hollow-sounding when tapped on bottom. If it browns too quickly, tent with aluminum foil during last 10 minutes of baking. Transfer bread to wire rack to cool. Garnish with star-shaped candies, if you wish.
Yield: Makes 16 servings.

PEANUT SESAME BRITTLE

- 2 tablespoons corn syrup
- 1¹/₂ cups sugar
- 1 tablespoon unsalted butter
- 1¹/₄ cups salted peanuts
- ¹/₄ cup sesame seeds

1. Coat a large baking sheet with nonstick vegetable-oil cooking spray.
2. Combine corn syrup, sugar and butter in large skillet over medium heat. Cook, swirling pan, until sugar is dissolved and turns golden brown, about 10 minutes.
3. Stir in peanuts and sesame seeds. Pour onto prepared baking sheet. Using back of metal spoon and working quickly, spread out nut mixture evenly. Cool completely. Break brittle into pieces. Store in airtight tins up to 2 months. To give as gifts, package in glass jars.
Yield: Makes 16 servings.

SHORTBREAD

- 2 cups all-purpose flour
- $1/2$ cup sugar
- $1/2$ teaspoon salt
- 1 cup (2 sticks) unsalted butter, at room temperature 1 hour, cut into 16 pieces (see Note)

1. Position oven rack in lower third of oven. Heat oven to 325°.
2. Place flour, sugar and salt in food processor. Whirl 5 seconds. Scatter butter pieces over mixture. Whirl until dough forms ball, 1 to 2 minutes. (Or cut in butter with pastry blender or fingertips.) Divide dough in half. Press each half evenly into 9-inch pie plate. Score each plate into 8 equal pie-shaped wedges.
3. Bake in lower third of 325° oven for 40 minutes. Cool pans on racks 5 minutes. Cut through scored marks. Cool before removing from pan.

Yield: Makes 16 pieces.

Note: For this rich cookie, butter is the preferred fat.

Chocolate Chip Shortbread: Add $1/4$ cup unsweetened cocoa powder to dry ingredients. Increase sugar to $2/3$ cup. After dough forms a ball, remove to bowl. Mix in $1/2$ cup mini chocolate chips. Press mixture into 9-inch square baking pan. Score into 36 pieces. (For thinner shortbread, use a 13 x 9-inch pan.) Bake in lower third of 325° oven for 45 minutes (or 40 minutes for larger pan). Cut through scored marks as above.

Yield: Makes 36 pieces.

Linzer Shortbread: Divide dough in half. Divide each half into 18 equal portions. Roll each portion into a smooth ball. Keeping edges as even as possible, press each ball into circle with 2-inch diameter. Make a deep impression with your thumb in center of each circle. Using a total of $1/2$ cup sliced almonds, press almonds evenly around depressions. Bake in lower third of 325° oven for 25 minutes. Remove pan from oven. Spoon $1/4$ teaspoon seedless raspberry jam in each depression. Return to oven. Bake 10 minutes longer. Sprinkle confectioners' sugar over cookies.

Yield: Makes 36 pieces.

STREUSEL-TOPPED BANANA BREAD

- $1^{1}/2$ cups all-purpose flour
- $1^{1}/2$ teaspoons baking powder
- $3/4$ teaspoon baking soda
- $1/4$ teaspoon salt
- $1/4$ teaspoon ground nutmeg
- $1/4$ ground cinnamon
- 1 cup mashed bananas (3 small overripe bananas, about 1 pound)
- 2 eggs
- $1/3$ cup sugar
- $1/4$ cup ($1/2$ stick) butter, melted

Streusel:

- $1/2$ cup all-purpose flour
- $1/2$ cup packed light-brown sugar
- $1/4$ cup ($1/2$ stick) butter, softened
- $1/2$ teaspoon ground nutmeg
- $1/2$ teaspoon ground cinnamon

1. Heat oven to 350°. Grease three $5^{3}/4$ x $3^{1}/4$ x 2-inch disposable mini-loaf pans.
2. Mix together flour, baking powder, baking soda, salt, nutmeg and cinnamon in medium-size bowl.
3. Beat bananas, eggs, sugar and butter in large bowl until smooth. On low speed, gradually beat in flour mixture. Divide batter among prepared pans.

Share a blissful assortment of Shortbread (above, left). *Streusel-Topped Banana Bread* (above, right) *will stir up fond memories of the classic loaf.*

4. Prepare Streusel: Mix flour, brown sugar, butter, nutmeg and cinnamon in bowl with fork until crumbly. Sprinkle over batter.

5. Bake in 350° oven for 30 minutes or until wooden pick inserted in centers comes out clean. If streusel is browning too quickly, cover loosely with foil. Cool cakes in pans on wire rack for 10 minutes. Remove cakes from pans to racks to cool completely.

Yield: Makes 3 mini loaves.

ORANGE-PINEAPPLE FRUIT SPREAD

- 2 packets unflavored gelatin
- 1/4 cup water
- 2 oranges
- 1 can (20 ounces) crushed pineapple, drained
- 1 can (12 ounces) frozen white grape juice concentrate
- 1 can (12 ounces) frozen apple juice concentrate
- 1 can (6 ounces) frozen orange juice concentrate
- 1 package (1 3/4 ounces) pectin

1. Soften gelatin in 1/4 cup water in small bowl, about 5 minutes.

2. Cut peel from oranges, removing all bitter white pith. Divide into sections; remove and discard membranes and seeds. Finely chop sections.

3. Combine oranges, pineapple, grape, apple and orange juice concentrates and pectin in medium-size, nonreactive saucepan. Bring to boiling. Remove from heat. Stir in gelatin until dissolved. Cool to room temperature. Cover; refrigerate for at least 24 hours before using.

4. Spoon into sterilized glass jars. Refrigerate up to 2 weeks.

Yield: Makes 5 cups.

PEAR AND CRANBERRY CONSERVE

- 3 pears, peeled, cored and chopped
- 1/4 cup sugar
- 1/4 cup light corn syrup
- 2 tablespoons fresh lemon juice
- 1 teaspoon ground ginger
- 1/8 teaspoon ground cloves
- 1 cup dried cranberries

1. Combine pears, sugar, corn syrup, lemon juice, ginger and cloves in large nonreactive saucepan. Bring to boiling over medium heat. Cook, stirring occasionally, until mixture thickens, about 20 minutes.

2. Stir in dried cranberries; cook 5 minutes. Remove from heat. Spoon into sterilized glass jars; cover.

3. Refrigerate for up to 2 weeks.

Yield: Makes 3 cups.

FRUIT-AND-NUT POPCORN BALLS

- 8 cups freshly popped popcorn
- 1/2 cup salted peanuts
- 1/2 cup dark raisins
- 1/4 cup firmly packed light-brown sugar
- 1/3 cup light corn syrup
- 1/2 teaspoon ground allspice
- 1/4 teaspoon salt
- 6 tablespoons (3/4 stick) unsalted butter, cut into pieces
- 1 teaspoon vanilla

1. Combine popcorn, peanuts and raisins in a 13 x 9 x 3-inch baking pan.

2. Heat oven to 350°. Combine brown sugar, corn syrup, allspice and salt in heavy medium saucepan. Add butter to pan; bring to boil over medium heat, stirring. Cook 5 minutes, stirring occasionally. Remove from heat and stir in vanilla. Pour glaze over popcorn mixture; toss with metal spoon until coated evenly.

3. Bake in 350° oven for 50 minutes, stirring every 15 minutes. Spoon into 16 mounds on waxed paper. With buttered hands, shape mounds into balls when cool enough to handle. (If mixture cools too quickly, rewarm it in oven 10 minutes or until soft enough to shape.) Store in airtight containers between sheets of waxed paper up to 1 month.

Yield: Makes 16 balls.

Breakfast-in-a-Bowl (below) beckons with pancake and muffin mixes plus Orange-Pineapple Fruit Spread and Pear and Cranberry Conserve. Wrap individual Fruit-and-Nut Popcorn Balls (not shown) in waxed paper squares and tie closed with cord or ribbon.

Every delicious slice of candy-sprinkled Cardamom-Walnut Pound Cake is sure to be devoured. Is your Christmas list longer than usual? Try splitting the batter into loaf pans for double the gift-giving. Soup up a friend's holiday with a Bottle O' Beans Mix (opposite, left) and a savory side dish of Herb-Marinated Cheese and Olives. The beans and their seasonings are key ingredients of Vegetable Minestrone Soup (not shown). It takes major willpower to stop after just a few Candied Almonds (opposite, right); handfuls are more like it.

CARDAMOM-WALNUT POUND CAKE

- 2 cups all-purpose flour
- 1 tablespoon ground cardamom
- 1/2 teaspoon salt
- 2 cups finely chopped walnuts
- 1 cup (2 sticks) unsalted butter or margarine, at room temperature
- 2 cups granulated sugar
- 1 tablespoon vanilla
- 7 eggs
- 1/2 cup milk
- 1 1/2 cups confectioners' sugar
- 2 tablespoons milk
  Candy sprinkles, for garnish (optional)

1. Heat oven to 325°. Grease and flour 10-inch Bundt pan (see Note).

2. Combine 1/2 cup flour, cardamom, salt and walnuts in a bowl.

3. Beat butter in large bowl on medium-high speed until smooth and creamy, about 2 minutes. Add granulated sugar; beat until fluffy, about 5 minutes. Beat in vanilla.

4. Beat in eggs, one at a time, beating about 30 seconds after each addition. Fold in remaining flour, nut mixture and 1/2 cup milk. Pour batter into prepared pan.

5. Bake in 325° oven for 1 hour 20 to 30 minutes or until wooden pick inserted in center comes out clean.

6. Remove to wire rack and cool 15 minutes. Invert cake onto wire rack and cool completely.

7. When cake is cooled, beat together confectioners' sugar and 2 tablespoons milk in bowl until smooth. Pour over cake. Garnish with candy sprinkles, if you wish.

Yield: Makes 16 servings.

Note: This cake may also be made in two 8 1/2 x 4 1/2 x 2 3/4-inch loaf pans; bake for about 1 hour 20 minutes. If using disposable aluminum baking pans approximately the same size, bake for about 1 hour 30 minutes.

BOTTLE O' BEANS MIX

Bean and Pea Mixture:

    1 cup dried kidney beans
    1 cup dried chickpeas
 1/2 cup dried navy beans
 1/2 cup dried black beans
 1/2 cup red lentils
 1/2 cup split peas

Seasoning Packet:

 1/2 cup dried parsley
 1/2 cup chicken-bouillon
     granules
    8 teaspoons dried leaf basil
    4 teaspoons dried leaf oregano
 1/4 teaspoon dried red-pepper flakes
     (optional)

Carefully layer beans and peas, 1 type at a time in 4-cup decorative bottle or jar. Add more beans, if needed; cork or seal. Place parsley, bouillon, basil, oregano and red-pepper flakes, if using, in small plastic bag; seal. Attach recipe for making Vegetable Minestrone Soup, below.
Yield: Makes 4 recipes of soup.

VEGETABLE MINESTRONE SOUP

    1 cup Bean and Pea Mixture
 1/4 cup plus 1 tablespoon seasoning
     from Seasoning Packet
   10 cups water
    5 cups cubed assorted vegetables,
     such as onions, sweet
     peppers, turnips, carrots,
     potatoes and celery
 1/2 cup small shaped pasta, such as
     elbow or mini bow tie
    2 teaspoons salt

1. Combine all beans and peas from gift bottle in a bowl. Pick over beans. Remove 1 cup beans, saving the remaining for additional recipes of soup. Soak beans overnight in water to cover; drain and rinse.
2. Combine beans, seasoning from packet and water in stockpot. Bring to simmering; cook, covered, 1 hour. Add vegetables, pasta and salt. Cook, covered, 20 minutes or until vegetables and beans are tender.
Yield: Make about 12 cups.

HERB-MARINATED CHEESE AND OLIVES

    2 cups olive oil
    2 tablespoons fresh rosemary
     leaves
    2 tablespoons fresh oregano
     leaves
    1 large clove garlic
 1/4 teaspoon dried red-pepper
     flakes
    2 packages (9 ounces each)
     miniature fresh mozzarella
     balls OR 1-pound package
     mozzarella, cut into 1-inch
     cubes
    1 cup oil-cured black olives
    6 sprigs fresh rosemary
    6 sprigs fresh oregano

1. In blender, whirl olive oil, rosemary leaves, oregano leaves, garlic and red-pepper flakes for 1 minute.
2. In clean pint jars, place mozzarella balls or cubes and olives. Arrange rosemary sprigs and oregano sprigs against sides of jars.
3. Spoon oil mixture into jars, covering cheese and olives. Cover with tight-fitting lids. Refrigerate for at least 2 days or for up to 2 weeks.
Yield: Makes three 1-pint jars.

CANDIED ALMONDS

 1 1/2 cups sugar
    1 egg white
 1 1/2 teaspoons vanilla
 1/8 teaspoon salt
    2 cups whole unblanched almonds

1. Heat oven to 300°. Line large baking sheet with aluminum foil.
2. Place sugar in large bowl.
3. Beat egg white lightly in medium-size bowl. Stir in vanilla and salt. Add almonds, tossing until coated with egg mixture.
4. Using a slotted spoon, transfer almonds to sugar in bowl; toss well to coat almonds evenly. Remove coated almonds to prepared baking sheet, spacing almonds 1/2 inch apart.
5. Bake in 300° oven for 20 to 25 minutes or until almonds are golden. Cool almonds completely on baking sheet. Store in airtight containers for up to 1 month.
Yield: Makes 5 cups.

Lace a batch of Spiked Truffle Stars (below) with a friend's favorite liqueur. Or gather a sampling of these rich variations for them to try (opposite, clockwise from top): Bittersweet Chocolate, White Chocolate, White-Cappuccino and Peanut Butter.

SPIKED TRUFFLE STARS

Try substituting a favorite flavored liqueur, such as almond, coffee, orange or raspberry, for the brandy.

- 10 squares (1 ounce each) semisweet chocolate
- 2 squares (1 ounce each) unsweetened chocolate
- 1/2 cup (1 stick) butter, softened
- 1 carton (8 ounces) reduced-cholesterol liquid whole eggs
- 2 tablespoons brandy
- 1 teaspoon vanilla

1. Line 2 large baking sheets with foil. Combine both chocolates in top of double boiler over hot, not boiling, water; stir occasionally, until melted and smooth.
2. Add butter, liquid eggs, brandy and vanilla, beating with whisk until smooth.
3. Place mixture over ice-water bath; chill 5 to 10 minutes, stirring occasionally, until frostinglike consistency but still smooth and creamy.
4. Spoon chocolate mixture into pastry bag fitted with large, fine star tip. Pipe 1-inch-diameter stars onto prepared baking sheets. Repeat with any mixture remaining in top of double boiler, whisking occasionally if mixture starts to harden. Refrigerate truffle stars for several hours or until hard enough to loosen from sheet and handle.
5. Store candies in tightly covered tin in refrigerator up to 1 week. Let come to room temperature to serve. Truffle stars can be frozen between sheets of waxed paper in tightly sealed container up to 1 month.
Yield: Makes about 7 dozen truffles.

BITTERSWEET CHOCOLATE TRUFFLES

- 1/2 cup heavy cream
- 8 squares (1 ounce each) bittersweet chocolate, chopped
- 1 tablespoon unsalted butter
- 1/2 teaspoon vanilla
  Cocoa powder

1. In medium-size saucepan, heat cream until mixture begins to simmer. Remove from heat, and stir in chocolate. Let stand for 5 minutes.
2. Add butter and vanilla; stir until smooth. Cover; refrigerate for at least 3 hours. By rounded measuring teaspoonfuls, scoop mixture onto waxed paper. Roll into balls, coating hands with cocoa powder, if needed.
3. Roll in cocoa powder to coat; chill, covered, for at least 2 hours. Store in airtight container for up to 2 weeks.
Yield: Makes about 2 dozen truffles.

Milk Chocolate Truffles: Prepare truffles as directed above, substituting milk chocolate for bittersweet chocolate.
Candied Ginger Truffles: Prepare truffles as directed above, adding 2 to 3 tablespoons finely chopped candied ginger in Step 2.

WHITE CHOCOLATE TRUFFLES

- 1/3 cup heavy cream
- 1 teaspoon fresh grated lemon zest
- 8 squares (1 ounce each) white chocolate, chopped
- 1 tablespoon unsalted butter
- 1/2 teaspoon vanilla
  Confectioners' sugar OR finely grated white chocolate, for coating

1. In medium-size saucepan, heat cream and lemon zest until mixture begins to simmer. Remove from heat; stir in chopped white chocolate. Let stand 5 minutes.
2. Add butter and vanilla; stir until smooth. Cover and refrigerate for at least 3 hours. By rounded measuring teaspoonfuls, scoop mixture onto waxed paper. Roll into balls, coating hands with confectioners' sugar, if needed.
3. Roll in confectioners' sugar to coat; chill, covered, for at least 2 hours. Store in airtight container for up to 2 weeks.
Yield: Makes about 2 dozen truffles.
Cherry Cream Truffles: Prepare truffles as directed above, adding 1/4 cup chopped candied cherries in Step 2. Roll in chopped pistachios, if desired.
Coconut Cream Truffles: Prepare truffles as directed above, omitting lemon zest and adding 1/3 cup chopped flaked coconut and 1/4 teaspoon coconut extract in Step 2. Roll in coconut, if desired.
Apricot Truffles: Soak 1/3 cup finely chopped apricots in 1 tablespoon brandy or orange liqueur for 15 minutes; drain, if needed. Prepare truffles as directed above, adding the brandied apricots in Step 2.

WHITE-CAPPUCCINO TRUFFLES

- $1/2$ cup heavy cream
- 2 teaspoons instant-espresso powder
- 8 squares (1 ounce each) white chocolate, chopped
- 1 tablespoon unsalted butter
- $1/2$ teaspoon vanilla
- $1/3$ cup confectioners' sugar OR 12 squares (1 ounce each) white chocolate, melted, for coating
- 24 small chocolate-coated espresso beans (optional)

1. In small saucepan, heat cream and espresso powder until almost simmering. Add chopped white chocolate and butter. Remove from heat; let stand for 5 minutes. Add vanilla, and stir until smooth. Cover; refrigerate for at least 3 hours.

2. By rounded measuring teaspoonfuls, scoop mixture onto waxed paper. Roll mixture into balls, coating hands with confectioners' sugar, if needed.

3. Roll in confectioners' sugar or dip into melted white chocolate. Garnish each truffle with 1 small chocolate-coated espresso bean, if desired.
Yield: Makes about 2 dozen truffles.

PEANUT BUTTER TRUFFLES

- $1/3$ cup heavy cream
- 8 squares (1 ounce each) white chocolate, chopped
- $1/2$ cup smooth peanut butter
- 1 tablespoon unsalted butter
- $1/2$ cup finely chopped peanuts OR $1/2$ cup confectioners' sugar

1. In medium-size saucepan, heat cream until almost simmering. Add chopped white chocolate and let stand for 5 minutes. Stir in peanut butter and butter until smooth.

2. Cover and refrigerate for at least 3 hours. By rounded measuring teaspoonfuls, scoop mixture onto waxed paper. Roll into balls, coating hands with confectioners' sugar, if needed.

3. Roll in peanuts or confectioners' sugar; chill for at least 2 hours. Store in airtight container for up to 3 weeks.
Yield: Makes about 2 dozen truffles.

CLAY BOTTLE STOPPERS

You need: Polymer clay; corks; acrylic paints; paintbrushes; craft glue.
To do: Fashion clay into desired shape. Carve away center until a cork can be inserted; then remove cork. Bake clay as per package directions. When cool, paint; glue cork inside stopper.

ORANGE-GINGER BISCOTTI

- 1 cup unsifted all-purpose flour
- 1 teaspoon baking powder
- 1/4 teaspoon salt
- 6 tablespoons (3/4 stick) butter, at room temperature
- 1/2 cup sugar
- 1 egg
- 1 egg yolk
- 1/2 teaspoon vanilla
- 3/4 cup coarsely chopped blanched almonds
- 3 tablespoons candied ginger, chopped
- 2 teaspoons grated orange zest
- 6 squares (1 ounce each) bittersweet OR semisweet chocolate

1. Heat oven to 350°. Lightly grease large baking sheet.
2. Stir together flour, baking powder and salt in a small bowl.
3. Beat butter and sugar in bowl until creamy. Beat in egg, yolk and vanilla.
4. Gradually beat flour mixture into butter mixture until smooth. Stir in almonds, ginger and orange zest.
5. On floured board or cloth, with floured hands, roll dough into cylinder about 1 1/2 inches in diameter. Transfer to prepared baking sheet.
6. Bake in 350° oven for 25 to 30 minutes or until wooden pick inserted in center comes out clean. Remove to wire rack; cool 20 minutes.
7. Using thin serrated knife, cut roll diagonally into 1/2-inch-wide pieces. Place on ungreased baking sheet.
8. Bake in 350° oven for 10 to 15 minutes or until golden. Cool on rack.
9. Melt chocolate in top of double boiler over hot water. Dip biscotti ends in chocolate; shake off excess. Place biscotti on waxed paper until firm.
Yield: Makes about 12 cookies.

HAZELNUT-CHOCOLATE CORDIAL

- 1 1/2 cups hazelnuts (about 1/2 pound)
- 3 cups vodka
- 1 vanilla bean, split lengthwise
- 3 tablespoons unsweetened cocoa powder
- 1 1/3 cups sugar
- 2/3 cup water
- 1 1/2 teaspoons (vegetable) glycerine (see Note)
- 1/8 teaspoon almond extract

1. Heat oven to 350°. Spread hazelnuts on large baking sheet and roast in 350° oven for 10 to 15 minutes or until skins split open and nuts are golden. Rub hazelnuts in clean kitchen towel to remove skins (some skin may remain). Cool nuts; coarsely chop.
2. Combine nuts, vodka and vanilla bean in quart jar with tight-fitting lid. Seal; let rest in cool place for at least 1 week or up to 1 month.
3. Strain vodka, pressing nuts to extract liquid (about 2 1/2 cups). Discard nuts. Return liquid to jar.
4. Stir cocoa powder into vodka; seal jar and shake well to combine. Let rest, undisturbed, in cool place for at least 1 week or up to 2 weeks.
5. Carefully ladle out translucent liquid from jar, leaving behind thick sludge. Strain translucent liquid through paper coffee filter (you should have about 2 to 2 1/4 cups).
6. Combine sugar and water in small saucepan. Bring to boiling over high heat, stirring until sugar is completely dissolved. Let cool to room temperature. Stir into vodka. Stir in glycerine and almond extract. Pour into clean, decorative bottles and set aside for at least 1 month.
Yield: Makes about 3 cups.
Note: Glycerine is available in stores selling wine-making equipment.

You'll have plenty of time to mold intriguing clay bottle stoppers in three holiday motifs — a pretty package, a frosty snowman and a colorful tree — while your gift of Hazelnut-Chocolate Cordial ages. Include a box or tin of luscious Orange-Ginger Biscotti for an extra helping of holiday cheer.

For spooning over ice cream or cake, a jar of Brandied Peaches (from left), Prunes in Port or Tarragon Pears makes an ideal gift for someone who likes to entertain. Any host or hostess will appreciate having such a convenient, impressive dessert in the pantry.

TARRAGON PEARS

   6 four-inch sprigs fresh tarragon OR 1^1/$_2$ tablespoons leaf tarragon
1^1/$_2$ cups granulated sugar
1^1/$_2$ cups packed light-brown sugar
1^1/$_2$ cups cider vinegar
1^1/$_2$ cups water
   8 pounds firm, ripe pears, peeled, cored and halved lengthwise
   6 sprigs fresh tarragon

1. If using dried tarragon, wrap in cheesecloth. In large nonreactive Dutch oven, combine tarragon, sugars, vinegar and water. Bring to a simmer; cook 5 minutes. Put pears in water to cover, to avoid discoloring.
2. Meanwhile, sterilize 6 clean 1-pint jars by boiling in water to cover for 5 minutes.
3. Add one-third of pears, and cook for 5 to 10 minutes or until just barely fork-tender. Into 2 jars, spoon pears; add 1 sprig tarragon to each. Repeat with remaining pears and tarragon. (Cooking in batches prevents pears from overcooking).
4. Add cooking liquid to jars to cover, filling within ^{1}/$_2$ inch of rims. Seal; process in hot-water bath for 15 minutes or refrigerate for up to 1 month.
Yield: Makes six 1-pint jars.

BRANDIED PEACHES

  10 small ripe peaches (about 3 pounds; see Note)
   2 cups sugar
   2 cups water
   6 whole cloves
  12 tablespoons peach schnapps OR apricot brandy
  18 cinnamon sticks

1. Dip peaches into boiling water for 30 seconds. Peel, halve and pit.
2. In medium-size saucepan, combine sugar, water and cloves. Bring to boil, then simmer for 5 minutes.
3. Add half of peaches to syrup; simmer for 5 minutes, and remove with slotted spoon to 3 hot, sterilized half-pint canning jars. Cover loosely. Repeat with remaining peaches and 3 jars. Boil syrup to reduce to about 1^1/$_2$ cups; discard cloves.
4. Add 2 tablespoons schnapps to each jar. Spoon in syrup, filling jars to within ^{1}/$_4$ inch of rim. Insert 3 cinnamon sticks down side of each jar.
5. Seal jars, following canning-jar manufacturer's directions; process in hot-water bath for 20 minutes. Remove; cool completely. Store in cool, dry place for up to 6 months. If you prefer not to process peaches, prepare as directed through Step 4; refrigerate for up to 2 weeks.
Yield: Makes six ^{1}/$_2$-pint jars.
Note: You may substitute 2 packages (20 ounces each) frozen dry-packed sliced peaches for fresh ones. Simmer for 2 minutes (instead of 5) in Step 3.

PRUNES IN PORT

   1 box (12 ounces) pitted prunes, about 42 prunes
   2 cups red port wine
   2 cups Beaujolais wine
   1 cup sugar
 ^{1}/$_2$ vanilla bean

1. In glass bowl, place prunes and port. Cover; refrigerate for 24 hours.
2. Wash 2 pint-size canning jars with lids and bands in hot soapy water. Rinse. Leave jars in clean, hot water until needed. Place lids and bands in saucepan of simmering water until needed.
3. Set prunes aside. Into medium-size saucepan, drain port. Add Beaujolais, sugar and vanilla bean to port. Bring to boiling over medium heat. Lower heat; simmer for 35 to 40 minutes or until reduced by one-third. Add prunes; return to boiling. Lower heat; simmer 1 minute. Discard vanilla bean.
4. Divide prunes and syrup into jars. Wipe jar rims and threads with damp cloth. Cover jars with hot lids; screw on bands firmly. Refrigerate for up to 3 months.
Yield: Makes two 1-pint jars.

A splendid FEAST

Whether you're **serving** buffet style — or sending kids to fetch extra chairs for a sit-down fete — you want Christmas dinner to look **splendid** and taste **sublime**.

GLAZED BABY CARROTS

2 tablespoons unsalted butter
1 pound baby carrots, peeled, cooked and drained
2 tablespoons fresh orange juice
1 tablespoon light-brown sugar
¼ teaspoon ground cinnamon
¼ teaspoon salt
⅛ teaspoon ground black pepper

Melt butter in skillet. Add cooked carrots, orange juice, brown sugar, cinnamon, salt and pepper. Cook, stirring, over high heat for 2 minutes or until glazed.
Yield: Makes 6 servings.

Either of our entrées — Roasted Pork Loin (opposite) or Thyme-Roasted Chicken (page 79) — makes a fine main dish. Festive Red-and-Green Salad and Glazed Baby Carrots (not shown) will never languish on the table.

ROASTED PORK LOIN

3 pound boneless loin of pork, trimmed
3 cloves garlic, thinly sliced
2 tablespoons fresh rosemary OR 2 teaspoons dried rosemary
2 tablespoons olive oil
1 teaspoon salt
¼ teaspoon ground black pepper

1. Heat oven to 350°. Make small slits with sharp knife on all sides of pork. Insert garlic and rosemary leaves into slits. Rub meat with olive oil. Sprinkle with salt and pepper. Place meat on a rack in roasting pan.
2. Roast in 350° oven until meat thermometer inserted in roast registers 160°, 1½ to 2 hours. Let stand 15 minutes before carving.
Yield: Makes 8 servings.

RED-AND-GREEN SALAD

2 sweet peppers (one red and one green), halved, cored, seeded and cut in ½-inch pieces
1 cucumber, peeled, halved, seeded and cut in ½-inch pieces
4 plum tomatoes, seeded and cut in ½-inch pieces
2 carrots, peeled and shredded
1 small bunch arugula, cut in 2-inch pieces
3 tablespoons olive oil
1 tablespoon balsamic vinegar
½ teaspoon salt
⅛ teaspoon ground black pepper

1. Combine red and green peppers, cucumber, tomatoes, carrots and arugula in bowl.
2. Whisk together olive oil, vinegar, salt and black pepper in a small bowl. Pour dressing over vegetables, tossing to coat. Serve chilled or at room temperature.
Yield: Makes 6 servings.

Our tasty side dishes of Broccoli Spears and Yellow Squash (clockwise from top left), Sweet Potato Salad and Potatoes Au Gratin match up perfectly. Golden-brown Thyme-Roasted Chicken (opposite) yields a savory broth for gravy.

SWEET POTATO SALAD

- 3 sweet potatoes (1³/₄ pounds), peeled and cut into ¹/₂-inch cubes
- 1 to 2 tablespoons fruit vinegar OR sherry vinegar
- 2 tablespoons vegetable oil
- ¹/₂ teaspoon salt
- ¹/₂ cup chopped hazelnuts
- ¹/₃ cup chopped, pitted dates

1. Place potatoes in large, shallow 3-quart microwave-safe dish. Cover with microwave-safe plastic wrap, vented at one corner. Microwave at full power (100%) for 12 minutes or until tender. Stir once. Cool slightly. (To prepare potatoes on stove top, cook in boiling water in saucepan for 8 to 10 minutes or until tender.) Drain.
2. Whisk vinegar, oil and salt in bowl. Add cooked potatoes, hazelnuts and dates. Toss gently. Serve warm.
Yield: Makes 6 servings.

POTATOES AU GRATIN

- 2 pounds Russet potatoes, peeled and thinly sliced
- 1 can (13³/₄ ounces) reduced-sodium chicken broth
- 3 tablespoons olive oil
- 3 tablespoons all-purpose flour
- 1¹/₂ cups low-fat milk (1%)
- 1 cup shredded Gruyère cheese
- 2 green onions, chopped
- ¹/₄ teaspoon salt
- ¹/₈ teaspoon ground black pepper
  Crumb Topping (recipe follows)

1. Heat oven to 350°. Butter 2-quart shallow casserole dish.
2. Place potatoes and broth in pot, adding water, if needed, to cover potatoes. Bring to a boil. Lower heat; simmer 5 minutes. Drain. Save broth for a soup. Transfer potatoes to bowl.
3. Heat olive oil in saucepan over low heat. Whisk in flour; cook 1 minute. Add milk. Cook, stirring, to thicken. Remove from heat. Stir in Gruyère, onions, salt and pepper. Add to potatoes; stir gently. Pour into casserole dish.
4. Bake in 350° oven for 45 minutes or until potatoes are tender. After first 30 minutes of baking, sprinkle on Crumb Topping.
Crumb Topping: Stir together 3 tablespoons plain packaged bread crumbs and 2 teaspoons olive oil.
Yield: Makes 6 servings.

BROCCOLI SPEARS AND YELLOW SQUASH

- 1 bunch broccoli
- 1 medium-size yellow squash
- 2 tablespoons olive oil
- 1 clove garlic, pressed
- ¹/₂ teaspoon dried leaf oregano
- ³/₄ teaspoon salt

1. Cut broccoli into spears. Halve squash lengthwise, then crosswise into ¹/₄-inch-thick half-moon slices. Steam broccoli and squash in a steamer basket in a covered large pot over gently boiling water until tender-crisp, about 10 minutes. Drain.
2. Whisk together olive oil, garlic, oregano and salt in serving bowl. Add vegetables to bowl. Toss and serve.
Yield: Makes 6 servings.

THYME-ROASTED CHICKEN

   6 **pound roasting chicken**
   1 **teaspoon salt**
  $^1/_2$ **teaspoon ground black pepper**
   2 **tablespoons melted butter**
   2 **tablespoons olive oil**
   2 **tablespoons chopped fresh thyme**
      OR 2 teaspoons dried thyme
      Gravy (recipe follows)

1. Heat oven to 350°. Remove giblets and neck from chicken. Discard. Rinse chicken in cool water. Pat dry with paper towels. Season inside and out with salt and pepper. Combine butter, olive oil and thyme in saucepan.
2. Fold neck skin under; fasten with skewer. Fold wings under back; tie legs and tail together. Insert meat thermometer in thickest part of thigh, without touching bone. Place, breast-side up, on rack in roasting pan. Brush with butter mixture.
3. Roast in 350° oven for 2 hours, basting, until thermometer registers 180°. Remove chicken to a cutting board. Let stand 20 minutes.
4. Prepare Gravy (recipe follows). Serve gravy with carved chicken.

Gravy: Pour pan drippings into glass measure. Skim off fat. Return 2 tablespoons drippings to pan. Whisk in 2 tablespoons flour and $^1/_2$ teaspoon dried thyme. Add enough water to drippings in measure to equal 2 cups. Gradually whisk into roasting pan. Cook, stirring and scraping up browned bits, until gravy thickens. Stir in $^1/_2$ teaspoon salt and $^1/_8$ teaspoon ground black pepper.
Yield: Makes 8 servings.

CHOCOLATE-NUT TART

 1$^1/_3$ **cups all-purpose flour**
   3 **tablespoons cocoa powder**
  $^1/_3$ **cup sugar**
  $^1/_4$ **teaspoon baking soda**
  $^1/_4$ **teaspoon salt**
  $^1/_3$ **cup unsalted butter, cut into slivers and chilled**
   1 **egg, lightly beaten**

Filling:
   3 **squares (1 ounce each) unsweetened chocolate**
   3 **tablespoons unsalted butter**
   1 **cup light corn syrup**
  $^1/_2$ **cup sugar**
   3 **eggs, lightly beaten**
   1 **teaspoon hazelnut liqueur (optional)**
  $^1/_2$ **teaspoon vanilla**
   1 **cup toasted hazelnuts, skinned and chopped (see Note)**
      Whipped cream and hazelnuts, for garnish

1. Combine flour, cocoa powder, sugar, baking soda and salt in bowl. Cut in butter with a pastry blender or 2 knives until mixture resembles coarse meal. Stir in egg with a fork until mixture holds together. Shape into a disk, wrap in plastic wrap and refrigerate 1 hour.
2. Heat oven to 350°. Butter a 9-inch pie pan or tart pan with removable bottom.
3. Place dough in pan; press evenly over bottom and up sides, extending dough $^1/_4$ inch above edge. Prick sides and bottom with a fork. Place in freezer for 10 minutes. Bake crust in 350° oven for 15 minutes; cool on a wire rack.
4. Prepare Filling: Melt chocolate and butter in a small saucepan over low heat; stir well. Let cool.
5. Bring corn syrup and sugar to a boil in a small saucepan, stirring. Lower heat; simmer 3 minutes. Cool. Mix in chocolate mixture. Whisk in eggs, hazelnut liqueur and vanilla.
6. Scatter nuts over bottom of crust. Pour chocolate mixture over nuts.
7. Bake in 350° oven for 25 minutes; filling should shake slightly in the center; cool on a wire rack. If using tart pan, remove sides of pan. Decorate top of tart with whipped cream rosettes and whole hazelnuts.
Yield: Makes 10 servings.
Note: To toast nuts, spread in a single layer on pan. Bake in 375° oven until toasted, 10 minutes. Cool slightly. Rub in a cloth towel to remove skins.

Our Strawberry and White Chocolate Cake is lavished with cream cheese frosting. Folks will be sorry if they don't save room for it — and for the Orange Tiramisu (opposite) and Chocolate-Nut Tart (recipe, page 79)!

STRAWBERRY AND WHITE CHOCOLATE CAKE

- 2 cups all-purpose flour
- 1 tablespoon baking powder
- 1 teaspoon salt
- 1 cup granulated sugar
- ¹/₂ cup butter or margarine, at room temperature
- 2 eggs
- ³/₄ cup milk
- 1 teaspoon almond extract

Filling:

- 5 squares (1 ounce each) white chocolate, coarsely chopped
- ¹/₃ cup heavy cream
- ²/₃ cup confectioners' sugar
- ¹/₄ cup strawberry jelly

Frosting:

- 6 squares (1 ounce each) white chocolate, coarsely chopped
- 1 package (8 ounces) cream cheese, at room temperature
- 1 tablespoon unsalted butter or margarine, at room temperature
- 1¹/₂ cups confectioners' sugar

Garnish:

- ¹/₂ cup sliced almonds
- 1 pint ripe strawberries

1. Heat oven to 350°. Grease a 15¹/₂ x 10¹/₂-inch jelly-roll pan. Line pan with waxed paper. Grease paper.
2. Combine flour, baking powder and salt. Beat sugar and butter in bowl until creamy. Add eggs, beating after each addition. On low speed, beat in flour mixture alternately with milk. Stir in extract. Spread batter into pan.
3. Bake in 350° oven for 25 minutes or until wooden pick inserted in center

comes out clean. Place pan on rack to cool completely. Cut crosswise into three 10 x 5-inch rectangles. Invert cake onto a work surface. Peel off paper.
4. Prepare Filling: Combine white chocolate and cream in top of double boiler over hot, not boiling, water. Stir until smooth. Beat in confectioners' sugar. Spread top of one cake layer with half of chocolate filling. Spread top of second layer with half of jelly. Place layer, jelly-side down, on first layer. Spread remaining filling over top of second layer. Spread remaining jelly over top of third layer; place layer, jelly-side down, on second layer. Chill. Trim edges even with knife.
5. Prepare Frosting: Melt chocolate in top of double boiler, stirring, over simmering, not boiling, water. Beat cream cheese and butter until smooth. Add melted chocolate and confectioners' sugar; beat until smooth.
6. Spread frosting over sides and top. Refrigerate 30 minutes. Garnish with almonds and strawberries. Refrigerate overnight before slicing.
Yield: Makes 12 servings.

ORANGE TIRAMISU

- 1 package (10³/₄ ounces) frozen pound cake, thawed
- 1 cup orange juice
- 1 package (3.4 ounces) instant vanilla pudding
- 2 cups milk
- 1 cup heavy cream, whipped
- 2 teaspoons grated orange zest
- 1 teaspoon orange extract
  Chocolate curls, orange zest and cocoa powder, for garnish

1. Cut cake crosswise into ¹/₂-inch-thick slices. Brush slices on both sides with orange juice.
2. Whisk together pudding mix and milk in bowl for 1 minute. Fold in whipped cream, orange zest and orange extract.
3. Spoon a thin layer of pudding mixture in shallow 2-quart serving dish. Arrange half of cake slices on top. Spread on half of pudding mixture. Repeat with remaining cake and pudding. Refrigerate 3 hours. Garnish with chocolate curls and orange zest strips. Sift cocoa powder over top.
Yield: Makes 8 servings.

MAKE-AHEAD CASSEROLES

the **holiday rush** can mean zero time to cook! But these wonderfully cozy **one-pot** suppers — all easy make-aheads — let you feed family and friends **deliciously** with no fuss at all!

MACARONI AND FOUR-CHEESE CASSEROLE

- 12 ounces elbow macaroni
- $1/2$ cup all-purpose flour
- $3^{1/4}$ cups milk
- $1/2$ teaspoon salt
- $1/4$ teaspoon ground nutmeg
- 1 cup shredded sharp Cheddar cheese (4 ounces)
- 1 cup shredded Swiss cheese (4 ounces)
- 1 cup shredded provolone cheese (4 ounces)
- 2 ounces cream cheese
- 1 teaspoon Dijon-style mustard

1. Heat oven to 350°. Coat $2^{1/2}$-quart baking dish with nonstick vegetable-oil cooking spray.
2. Cook elbow macaroni following package directions. Drain.
3. Whisk flour and 1 cup milk in large saucepan until smooth. Stir in remaining milk, salt and nutmeg; cook, stirring constantly, over medium heat until thickened and bubbly, 2 minutes. Remove from heat. Stir in cheeses and mustard. Stir in macaroni. Pour into baking dish.
4. Bake in 350° oven for 30 minutes or until lightly browned and bubbly.
Yield: Makes 8 servings.

THREE-BEAN TAMALE PIE

- 2 tablespoons olive oil
- 1 package (10 ounces) frozen corn kernels, thawed
- 1 jalapeño pepper, seeded and finely chopped
- 1 teaspoon dried oregano
- 1 teaspoon ground cumin
- $1^{1/2}$ teaspoons salt
- $1/4$ teaspoon ground black pepper
- $2^{1/4}$ cups cold water
- 1 cup sliced green onions (green and white parts)
- $1/3$ cup chopped fresh cilantro
- 3 cups reduced-sodium chicken broth
- 2 cups yellow cornmeal
- 1 can (16 ounces) pink or pinto beans, drained and rinsed
- 1 can (16 ounces) kidney beans, drained and rinsed
- 1 can (16 ounces) black beans, drained and rinsed
- 2 cups shredded sharp Cheddar cheese (8 ounces)
- 1 can (28 ounces) tomatoes in juice, drained and coarsely chopped
- $1/4$ cup plain low-fat yogurt
- $1/4$ cup tomato sauce

1. Heat oil in large nonstick skillet over medium heat. Add corn; cook until browned, stirring often, about 8 minutes. Add jalapeño, oregano, cumin, $1/2$ teaspoon of salt and pepper; cook 1 minute. Pour $1/4$ cup of water into skillet; cook, scraping up any browned bits from bottom of skillet, until liquid evaporates, about 2 minutes. Remove from heat. Mix in green onions and cilantro.
2. Heat oven to 350°. Coat 12 x 7 x 2-inch or other $2^{1/2}$- to 3-quart baking dish with nonstick vegetable-oil cooking spray.
3. Bring chicken broth in saucepan to boiling. Stir together cornmeal and 2 cups cold water in bowl. When broth boils, add cornmeal mixture all at once, stirring constantly; cook, stirring, over medium heat until consistency of mashed potatoes, about 8 minutes. Add remaining 1 teaspoon salt. Cool slightly.
4. Spread two-thirds of cornmeal mixture in prepared dish. Combine beans in bowl. Spoon over cornmeal; press down lightly. Sprinkle with cheese, reserving $1/2$ cup.
5. Toss tomatoes with corn mixture; spread over cheese. Dab spoonfuls of remaining cornmeal mixture over top; it is not necessary to completely cover.
6. Combine yogurt and tomato sauce in a bowl; spoon in diagonal lines across top of casserole. Sprinkle with remaining $1/2$ cup cheese.
7. Bake in 350° oven for 1 hour or until top is browned and casserole is heated through. Let stand for 15 minutes before cutting.
Yield: Makes 12 servings.

The tasty Macaroni and Four-Cheese Casserole (top) and zesty Three-Bean Tamale Pie (bottom) are easy to make one day and serve the next. As the flavors meld, each casserole tastes better and better!

HENHOUSE CHICKEN POTPIES

Peppered Herb Pastry:

1¼ cups all-purpose flour
½ teaspoon dried oregano
½ teaspoon dried basil
½ teaspoon dried thyme
½ teaspoon salt
¼ teaspoon ground black pepper
⅓ cup vegetable shortening, chilled
2 tablespoons butter, chilled
2 to 4 tablespoons ice water

Filling:

1 medium-size potato, unpeeled and cut into ½-inch cubes
2 medium-size carrots, peeled and sliced
2 cups cooked, diced, boneless, skinned chicken breast (see Note)
1 cup frozen tiny peas
3 tablespoons chopped parsley
2 tablespoons butter
1 medium-size onion, chopped
1 large clove garlic, finely chopped
½ teaspoon dried basil
⅛ teaspoon ground nutmeg
⅓ cup all-purpose flour
2 cups reduced-sodium chicken broth
¼ cup dry sherry OR dry white wine
¾ teaspoon ground black pepper
½ teaspoon salt

1. Prepare Peppered Herb Pastry: Combine flour, oregano, basil, thyme, salt and pepper in a bowl. Cut in shortening and butter with pastry blender until mixture resembles coarse meal. Sprinkle with 2 tablespoons ice water, tossing with a fork, until mixture comes together. Add more water, if necessary. Shape into a ball; flatten into a 6-inch round. Wrap in plastic wrap. Refrigerate at least 1 hour.
2. Prepare Filling: Bring 1½ quarts water to boiling in large saucepan. Drop in potato and carrots; boil 2 minutes. Drain. Combine with chicken, peas and parsley in a bowl.
3. Heat oven to 400°. Heat butter in saucepan. Add onion; sauté until softened, 4 minutes. Add garlic, basil and nutmeg; sauté 1 minute. Sprinkle flour over top; stir to blend. Whisk in broth, sherry, pepper and salt; cook, stirring, until thickened and bubbly. Add to chicken and vegetables. Divide filling equally among five 12-ounce ramekins or baking dishes.
4. Divide pastry into 5 equal pieces. On floured surface, with floured rolling pin, roll out each piece of pastry into a round 1 inch larger than top of ramekin. Trim and crimp edge. Prick top of crust. Place ramekins on baking sheet.
5. Bake in 400° oven for 40 to 50 minutes or until crust is browned and filling is bubbly; cover crust with aluminum foil if browning too quickly. Let stand 10 minutes before serving.
Yield: Makes 5 generous servings.

Note: A 1½-pound boneless chicken breast will yield 2 cups diced cooked chicken when poached. Cooking liquid can be used for broth in recipe.

MEATBALLS AND BOW TIES

1 pound bow tie pasta
2 tablespoons vegetable oil
8 cups lightly packed shredded green cabbage
2 tablespoons finely chopped fresh ginger
1 large clove garlic, finely chopped
1 teaspoon salt
1 teaspoon sugar
⅓ cup all-purpose flour
3 cups chicken broth
2 tablespoons tomato paste
1 tablespoon soy sauce
6 ounces cream cheese, at room temperature
¼ cup chopped fresh parsley

Meatballs:

¼ cup plain dry bread crumbs
½ cup milk
1 pound lean ground beef
3 ounces mushrooms, coarsely grated
1 egg
1½ tablespoons soy sauce

1. Cook bow ties following package directions. Drain; return to pot.
2. Meanwhile, heat oil in large nonstick skillet over medium-high heat. Add cabbage; cook, stirring often, until

browned and wilted, about 10 minutes. Stir in ginger, garlic, salt and sugar until well blended; cook for 2 minutes.

3. Sprinkle flour over cabbage; stir to mix. Add chicken broth, tomato paste and soy sauce; cook over medium heat, stirring constantly, until thickened and bubbly, about 3 minutes. Remove from heat. Stir in cream cheese and parsley until well blended. Stir cabbage mixture into bow ties.

4. Heat oven to 350°. Coat 3-quart baking dish with nonstick vegetable-oil cooking spray.

5. Meanwhile, prepare Meatballs: Combine bread crumbs and milk in bowl; let stand for 5 minutes for bread crumbs to soften. Mix in beef, mushrooms, egg and soy sauce. Shape into walnut-size meatballs.

6. Spoon about one-third of bow tie mixture into prepared baking dish. Place half of uncooked meatballs over bow ties. Repeat layers. Top with remaining bow tie mixture.

7. Bake, covered, in 350° oven for 45 to 55 minutes or until hot and meatballs are cooked through.

Yield: Makes 8 servings.

TURKEY-NOODLE CASSEROLE WITH SPINACH

12	ounces wide egg noodles
1	medium-size onion, chopped
1	tablespoon butter
1	large clove garlic, finely chopped
1	teaspoon dried oregano
1	teaspoon dried basil
1/4	teaspoon ground nutmeg
1	container (15 ounces) part-skim ricotta cheese
1	cup chicken broth
1	teaspoon salt
1/4	teaspoon ground black pepper
12	ounces cooked turkey breast, torn into 2 x 1/2-inch pieces (about 3 cups)
1	package frozen chopped spinach, thawed and squeezed dry
1/2	cup grated Parmesan cheese

1. Cook noodles following package directions. Drain.

2. Heat oven to 375°. Coat 2 1/2- to 3-quart baking dish with nonstick vegetable-oil cooking spray.

3. Sauté onion in butter in medium-size saucepan over medium heat until softened, about 3 minutes. Stir in garlic, oregano, basil and nutmeg; sauté for 1 minute. Remove saucepan from heat. Stir in ricotta until well blended. Stir in chicken broth, salt and pepper. Stir in turkey.

4. In a large bowl, combine cooked noodles, spinach, turkey mixture and all but 2 tablespoons of Parmesan cheese. Pour into baking dish. Cover with aluminum foil.

5. Bake in 375° oven for 15 minutes. Sprinkle top with remaining 2 tablespoons Parmesan cheese. Bake, uncovered, for 20 minutes.

Yield: Makes 6 servings.

SCALLOPED HAM AND POTATOES

3	pounds all-purpose potatoes
1 1/2	cups milk
1/3	cup all-purpose flour
1	cup half-and-half
3/4	cup water
1	packet (.19 ounce) vegetable broth powder
1	teaspoon dried thyme
1/2	teaspoon salt
1/4	teaspoon ground black pepper
12	ounces ham, diced
4	green onions, thinly sliced
1/2	cup shredded Swiss cheese

1. Bring large pot of water to boiling. Peel potatoes; thinly slice, placing slices in bowl of cold water as you slice. Drop drained slices into boiling water; boil 3 minutes. Drain.

2. Heat oven to 375°. Coat 2 1/2- to 3-quart baking dish with nonstick vegetable-oil cooking spray.

3. Stir together 1/2 cup milk and flour in medium-size saucepan until smooth. Stir in remaining 1 cup milk, half-and-half, water, vegetable broth powder, thyme, salt and pepper; cook, stirring, over medium heat until sauce thickens and bubbles, about 3 minutes.

4. Spoon one-third of potatoes into baking dish. Sprinkle with half of ham and green onions. Spoon on one-third of sauce. Repeat layers, ending with potatoes and remaining sauce.

5. Bake, covered, in 375° oven for 30 minutes. Sprinkle cheese over top. Bake, uncovered, 15 minutes or until lightly browned. Let stand 10 minutes before serving.

Yield: Makes 6 servings.

Turkey-Noodle Casserole With Spinach (top) is a palate-pleaser. Swiss cheese tops the Scalloped Ham and Potatoes (bottom). Henhouse Chicken Potpies (opposite, left) are rich with gravy. Meatballs and Bow Ties (opposite, right) have a touch of ginger for a nice surprise.

OLD WORLD
TRADITIONS

Christmas breads & cakes from Europe

Start your own **holiday** tradition and serve a dish that's long been in your family. These five European **breads and cakes** are delicious regional **favorites** reflecting the faith and legends of Christmas through the centuries.

KOLACH
Ukrainian Braided Bread Rings

- $1/3$ cup warm water (105° to 115°)
- 2 packages active dry yeast
- $2/3$ cup sugar
- $1/2$ cup milk
- 2 eggs
- 1 teaspoon vanilla
- $1/2$ teaspoon almond extract
- $5 1/2$ cups all-purpose flour
- 1 teaspoon salt
- $1/2$ cup (1 stick) unsalted butter, at room temperature
- $3/4$ cup chopped almonds
- 1 tablespoon grated orange zest
- 1 egg, beaten
  Poppy seeds
  Candied orange peel, for garnish (optional)

1. Stir together water, yeast and 1 teaspoon of sugar in 2-cup glass measure. Let stand 5 minutes or until foamy. Stir in milk, eggs, vanilla and almond extract.

2. Place flour, salt, butter, almonds, orange zest and remaining sugar in food processor. With machine running, gradually add yeast mixture. Process until mixture forms a ball (if mixture is too dry, add water, 1 tablespoon at a time; if too wet, add flour, 2 tablespoons at a time). Process 30 seconds more. Place in greased bowl, cover with a towel and let rise $1 1/2$ to 2 hours or until doubled.

3. Punch down dough. Turn out onto floured surface; roll into an 18-inch log. Cut into 8-inch, 6-inch and 4-inch pieces.

4. For base layer, divide the largest batch of dough into thirds. Roll 2 of the pieces into two 32-inch ropes; twist together. Place in a ring shape in greased 10-inch pan, leaving 1-inch space around edge. Moisten joining edges with water and pinch together to seal. Divide remaining piece in half, roll into two 26-inch ropes and twist together. Place in pan, inside the other bread ring. Moisten and pinch joining edges. Grease the outside of a large clean can or oven-proof canning jar and place in center of rings. (This will keep hole from closing up.)

5. For middle layer, using 6-inch piece of dough, repeat process, shaping ropes into pairs of 24- and 16-inch-long pairs, respectively, and forming into a 7-inch round. Place on greased baking sheet with medium greased jar in center. For smallest layer, using smallest piece of dough, repeat process, shaping ropes into 16- and 12-inch-long pairs, respectively, and forming into a 4-inch round. Place on greased baking sheet with small greased jar in center. Cover breads and let rise 1 to $1 1/2$ hours or until doubled.

6. Heat oven to 350°. Lightly brush breads with beaten egg and sprinkle with poppy seeds. Bake breads for 15 to 25 minutes, removing breads when golden and hollow sounding when tapped. Remove breads as they are cooked, starting with the smallest loaf. Remove jars from centers and place breads on racks to cool completely.

7. To serve, stack breads, starting with largest as the base. Garnish with candied orange peel and place a large candle in center, if you wish.

We added almonds and grated orange zest for a fragrant and flavorful variation on the customary kolach. But just as Ukrainians do, we baked three rings of bread, stacked them, then placed a candle in the center. The tiers are an ancient symbol of the Trinity, the rings (kolo means "circle" in Ukrainian) symbols of eternity.

For many, kolach is the highlight of a Christmas meal filled with reminders of the true meaning of the season. A family, for example, may put a little hay under the tablecloth and toss some on the floor to recall the manger and stable where Jesus was born. An extra place may be laid at the head of the table as a reminder that Christ is the unseen head of the household.

into a log. Knead gently into a ball. Flatten into a 6¹/₂-inch round. Place on greased baking sheet.

4. Roll 2 reserved strips into 21-inch ropes of even thickness; twist together and wrap around the base of disk. Brush joining rope ends with water and pinch to seal. Roll 2 remaining strips into 14-inch ropes. Using a sharp knife, split 4 inches of each rope end lengthwise.

5. Place remaining ropes on top, crossing in center. Curl split ends away from edge. Arrange walnut halves on top. Cover with a towel and let rise 1¹/₂ hours or until doubled.

6. Heat oven to 350°. Brush bread with egg white. Sprinkle top with coarse sugar. Bake for 30 to 35 minutes or until golden brown and hollow sounding when tapped. Cover with foil during last 10 minutes, if browning too quickly. Cool completely on rack. Can be frozen, wrapped airtight, for up to 3 months.
Yield: Makes 16 servings.

T his sweet, rich bread from southern Greece is traditionally topped with a Byzantine cross of dough and nuts, then sugar glazed. The christopsomo ("Christ's bread") is then placed in the center of the table on Christmas Eve and blessed by the head of the household. It's often served with fruit, nuts and perhaps a pot of honey. After dinner, a piece of the bread is sometimes left on the table in case Christ should come and eat during the night. Or a slice might be saved for the first needy person who comes to the house on Christmas Day.

Our adaptation of this treasured recipe calls for golden raisins, dried figs and chopped walnuts. It's wonderful served warm with coffee or tea.

CHRISTOPSOMO
Greek Christmas Eve Bread

¹/₄ cup warm water (105° to 115°)
1 package active dry yeast
¹/₃ cup granulated sugar
¹/₂ cup milk
1 egg
1 egg yolk
³/₄ cup all-purpose flour
³/₄ teaspoon salt
³/₄ teaspoon anise seed, chopped or crushed (optional)
1 teaspoon grated lemon zest
¹/₃ cup unsalted butter, at room temperature
¹/₂ cup chopped walnuts
¹/₂ cup golden raisins
¹/₃ cup chopped dried figs OR ¹/₃ cup dried apricots
8 walnut halves
1 egg white, lightly beaten
Coarse sugar

1. Stir together water, yeast and 1 teaspoon of granulated sugar in 2-cup glass measure. Let stand 5 minutes or until foamy. Stir in milk, egg and egg yolk.

2. Place flour, salt, anise seed, lemon zest, butter and remaining granulated sugar in food processor. With machine running, gradually add yeast mixture. Process until mixture forms a ball. (If mixture is too dry, add water, 1 tablespoon at a time; if too wet, add flour, 2 tablespoons at a time.) Process 30 seconds more. Place in greased bowl, cover with a towel and let rise 1¹/₂ to 2 hours or until doubled.

3. Turn out onto floured surface and flatten to a 14 x 11-inch rectangle. Cut off and set aside four 14 x ³/₄-inch strips of dough. Sprinkle walnuts, raisins and figs onto dough. Roll up from long side

Our sugar-coated little bread men are just like those sold in Swiss bakeries as St. Nicholas Day treats for good boys and girls.

Other countries in Europe and South America remember the patron saint of children on December 6 with similar bread dolls. Gifts are often exchanged on that day, and children are surprised with goodies left by the saint. Swiss *grättimannen* are thought to resemble the saint's helpers.

Though his many acts of compassion are the stuff of legend, there actually was a generous Bishop Nikolaos. Born to a wealthy Turkish family in the fourth century, he devoted his life to the church and the poor. It's said he left presents on the doorsteps of needy children at night, and so the tale of Santa was born.

GRÄTTIMANNEN
Swiss St. Nicholas Day Bread Dolls

- ¼ cup warm water (105° to 115°)
- 1 package active dry yeast
- ⅓ cup sugar
- ¼ cup milk
- 1 egg
- 3¼ cups all-purpose flour
- ¾ teaspoon ground cinnamon
- ¾ teaspoon salt
- ¼ cup (½ stick) unsalted butter, at room temperature
- 1 egg, beaten

1. Stir together water, yeast and 1 teaspoon of sugar in 2-cup glass measure. Let stand 5 minutes or until foamy. Stir in milk and egg.

2. Place flour, cinnamon, salt, butter and remaining sugar in food processor. With machine running, gradually add yeast mixture. Process until mixture forms a ball. (If mixture is too dry, add water, 1 tablespoon at a time; if too wet, add flour, 2 tablespoons at a time.) Process 30 seconds more. Place in greased bowl, cover with a towel and let rise 1½ to 2 hours or until doubled.

3. Turn out onto floured surface, shape into 12-inch rope and cut into six 2-inch pieces. Working with one piece of dough, use about half of dough to shape into body. Use remaining to shape head, arms and legs, adding as much detail as you wish (shoes, buttons, collars, etc.). Assemble dolls on greased baking sheets, 3 inches apart. Cover with a towel and let rise 1 to 1½ hours in a warm place or until doubled.

4. Heat oven to 350°. Brush dolls lightly with beaten egg. Bake for 17 to 20 minutes or until golden brown and hollow sounding when tapped. Cool on rack. Can be frozen, wrapped airtight, for up to 3 months.
Yield: Makes six 9-inch dolls.

A golden paper crown sits atop our light-as-air twist on this famous cake. Galette des Rois is served during the evening activities on the Feast of the Epiphany, January 6, the final day of the holy season in France. A single bean was once baked inside, but nowadays a porcelain good-luck charm or nut is the more likely symbol of the gifts of the magi. Traditionally, the fortunate person who finds the charm becomes the king or queen for the evening and may choose a royal court and lead the party games.

GALETTE DES ROIS
Cake of the Kings of France

2¹/₂ cups all-purpose flour
   1 teaspoon baking soda
1¹/₄ teaspoons baking powder
 ³/₄ teaspoon salt
 ³/₄ cup (1¹/₂ sticks) unsalted
        butter, at room temperature
1¹/₄ cups sugar
   4 eggs, separated
   2 tablespoons lemon juice
   1 cup milk
   1 pecan half or whole almond,
        shelled
       Confectioners' sugar

1. Heat oven to 325°. Grease and flour a 12-cup (10-inch) decorative tube mold (kugelhopf) or Bundt pan.
2. Combine flour, baking soda, baking powder and salt in medium bowl. Beat together butter and 1 cup sugar for 1 minute or until smooth.
3. Add egg yolks and lemon juice. Beat for 2 minutes or until light and fluffy. Add milk and half of flour mixture; beat until just combined.
4. Beat egg whites until very soft peaks form. Beat in remaining sugar until soft peaks form. Alternately fold in egg whites and remaining flour into yolk mixture in 2 additions until just combined. Pour into prepared pan. Place nut in center, pressing in slightly and covering with batter.
5. Bake in 325° oven for 45 to 50 minutes or until wooden pick inserted in center of cake comes out clean. Cool in pan on rack for 10 minutes; invert onto rack and cool completely.
6. Sprinkle with confectioners' sugar.
Yield: Makes 20 servings.

PAMPEPATO
Italy's Chocolate Christmas Cake

Marzipan Fruit:
- ³/₄ cup slivered almonds, finely ground
- 1³/₄ cups confectioners' sugar
- 1¹/₂ tablespoons water
- ¹/₂ teaspoon almond extract
  Peach, red, green and yellow paste food coloring
  Whole cloves and maraschino cherry stems, to decorate

Cake:
- ¹/₂ cup golden raisins
- 3 tablespoons brandy or rum
- 2 ounces unsweetened chocolate, finely chopped
- 1 cup honey
- ¹/₂ teaspoon crushed anise seed (optional)
- ³/₄ cup canned pear purée
- ¹/₄ cup unsalted butter, at room temperature
- 1 tablespoon grated orange zest
- 2¹/₂ cups all-purpose flour
- 1¹/₂ teaspoons baking soda
- 1 teaspoon ground cinnamon
- ¹/₄ teaspoon ground cloves
- 1¹/₂ cups toasted walnuts, finely chopped

Glaze:
- 1 cup heavy cream
- 8 squares (1 ounce each) semisweet chocolate, chopped
- 1 square (1 ounce) unsweetened chocolate, chopped

1. (**Note:** Make Marzipan Fruit a day before making cake.) Prepare Marzipan Fruit: Combine almonds, 1 cup confectioners' sugar, water and almond extract; beat until well blended. Beat in remaining confectioners' sugar.

2. Divide marzipan evenly into 4 bowls. Tint 1 bowl peach, 1 bowl red, 1 bowl light green and 1 bowl yellow by kneading in food coloring.

3. For each peach, shape peach marzipan to resemble a peach. Make a crease in peach with a knife. Insert cherry stem into top of peach; insert stem of clove into bottom.

4. For each apple, shape red marzipan to resemble an apple. Insert cherry stem into top of apple; insert stem of clove into bottom.

5. For each pear, shape green marzipan to resemble a pear. Insert cherry stem into top of pear; insert stem of clove into bottom.

6. For each lemon, shape yellow marzipan to resemble a lemon. Insert flat end of clove into bottom of lemon and lightly cover with marzipan.

7. In a small bowl, mix a small amount of red food coloring with water to make a thin paint. Repeat with yellow food coloring. Use a small, clean paintbrush to paint red shading on pears and peaches and yellow shading on apples.

8. Cover and chill fruit at least 1 day before decorating cake.

9. Prepare Cake: Heat oven to 325°. Grease and flour a 9-inch springform pan.

10. Bring raisins and brandy to simmer in small saucepan. Remove from heat, cover and let soak 30 minutes. Meanwhile, heat chocolate and half of honey in a medium saucepan until chocolate is melted, stirring until smooth. Remove from heat and stir in anise seed, pear purée, butter, orange zest and remaining honey.

11. Stir together flour, baking soda, cinnamon, cloves and walnuts in a large bowl. Make a well in the center, add honey mixture and stir together until combined. Pour into prepared pan.

12. Bake in 325° oven for 50 to 60 minutes or until wooden pick inserted in center of cake comes out clean. Cool in pan on rack for 15 minutes; remove sides from pan and cool on rack completely.

13. Prepare Glaze: Heat cream in heavy saucepan until bubbles form around side of pan. Remove from heat, add chocolates and stir until smooth. Let stand for 20 to 30 minutes or until thickened to a soft-frosting consistency.

14. Invert cake on rack set over jelly-roll pan. Glaze sides and top of cake with chocolate mixture, reapplying any extra glaze. Cool until glaze has hardened. Decorate with Marzipan Fruit.

Yield: Makes 20 servings.

The scrumptious chocolate-and-honey cake known as pampepato was created in the 15th century at the monastery of Corpus Domini in Ferrara, Italy. Some believe the cake's original name was pan del pape, or "bread of the pope."

In modern times, every pasticceria, or pastry shop, in Ferrara displays its own version of this elegant dessert during the holidays. Italians often present a pampepato to friends, in keeping with an ancient tradition that says a gift containing honey is sure to bring the recipient a new year filled with sweetness.

Our deliciously moist recipe is made with chocolate melted in honey, plus walnuts, raisins, pear purée and just a touch of brandy. The frosting is a luscious blend of chocolate and cream, and the fruits are marzipan.

COOKIE
countdown

Yummy aromas, new things to taste,
and batter, batter everywhere … at
holiday time the kitchen is the place
to be. Making a variety of sweets
can be easy … and we won't
tell if you don't.

BASIC HOLIDAY COOKIES

1¼ cups all-purpose flour
½ teaspoon baking powder
¼ teaspoon salt
3 tablespoons unsalted butter
3 tablespoons margarine
½ cup sugar
1 egg
½ teaspoon vanilla

1. Stir together flour, baking powder and salt in a small bowl.
2. Beat together butter, margarine and sugar in another bowl until creamy. Beat in egg and vanilla until well blended. Stir in flour mixture. Shape into a disk, wrap in plastic wrap and refrigerate several hours or overnight.
3. Heat oven to 350°. Coat baking sheets with nonstick vegetable-oil cooking spray.
4. Roll out dough on lightly floured surface to ³/₈-inch thickness. Cut into rounds with 2¹/₂-inch cookie cutter; reroll scraps. Place on prepared baking sheets, spacing 1¹/₂ inches apart.
5. Bake in 350° oven for 10 to 12 minutes or until lightly browned at edges. Remove cookies to wire rack to cool.
Yield: Makes about 2¹/₂ dozen cookies.

CHRISTMAS TREES

Prepare double recipe **Basic Holiday Cookie** dough. Roll out quarter of dough at a time on well-floured surface to ³/₁₆-inch thickness. Cut out trees with 5¹/₂-inch tree-shaped cookie cutter. Reroll scraps; cut out trees for total of 16. Bake on baking sheets coated with nonstick vegetable-oil cooking spray in 350° oven for 12 minutes or until lightly browned at edges. While still warm, cut 8 trees in half vertically. Cool on rack. Spread one side of cookies and edges with icing. Press on candy-coated chocolate candies. Let dry. Repeat with other sides. Let dry. Pipe band of icing down center of whole trees on both sides. Push half-tree into icing band on both sides. Hold until icing firms. Let dry. Dust tops with confectioners' sugar.
Yield: Makes 8 cookie trees.

DOUBLE CHOCOLATE BALLS

Prepare **Basic Holiday Cookie** dough, with the following changes: Substitute ¹/₄ cup packed brown sugar for granulated; add 2 tablespoons unsweetened cocoa powder to flour mixture. Wrap in plastic and refrigerate until well chilled. For each cookie, place mini chocolate kiss on ¹/₂ tablespoon of dough. Press dough around kiss to enclose completely. Place on baking sheets. Bake in 350° oven 10 to 12 minutes. While still warm, roll in granulated sugar. Cool on wire racks.
Yield: Makes about 3¹/₂ dozen cookies.

CITRUS STARS

Prepare **Basic Holiday Cookie** dough, with the following changes: Omit vanilla; add 1¹/₂ teaspoons *each* grated lemon and lime zest with egg. Wrap in plastic; refrigerate until well chilled. Roll out dough on floured surface, half at a time, to ³/₁₆-inch thickness. Cut out with star-shaped cookie cutters. Reroll scraps. Place on baking sheets coated with nonstick vegetable-oil cooking spray. Bake in 350° oven for 10 to 12 minutes. Cool on racks. Spread some stars with yellow Buttercream Frosting (page 95), remaining with white. Sprinkle with decorator sugar.
Yield: Makes about 1¹/₂ dozen.

PISTACHIO-CHOCOLATE PINWHEELS

Prepare **Basic Holiday Cookie** dough, with the following changes: Substitute ³/₄ teaspoon almond extract for vanilla; stir ¹/₂ cup finely chopped pistachio nuts and green food coloring into dough. Prepare a second recipe of **Basic Holiday Cookie** dough, with the following changes: Substitute ¹/₄ cup packed brown sugar for ¹/₄ cup granulated; add 2 tablespoons unsweetened cocoa powder to flour. Wrap doughs in plastic; refrigerate until chilled. Roll out half the chocolate dough on floured waxed paper to a 10 x 7-inch rectangle. Repeat with half the pistachio dough. Place pistachio dough on top of chocolate. Peel off top paper. Starting with long side, roll up doughs tightly, jelly-roll fashion, using bottom paper as guide and removing paper as you roll. Wrap; chill. Repeat with remaining doughs. Cut in ¹/₄-inch-thick slices. Place on baking sheets. Bake in 350° oven for 10 to 12 minutes. Cool on racks.
Yield: Makes about 7¹/₂ dozen cookies.

Turn our Basic Holiday Cookies recipe into a variety of goodies, like fruity Citrus Stars (top), Pistachio-Chocolate Pinwheels (bottom), Double Chocolate Balls (not shown), and 3-D Christmas Trees (opposite).

12 DAYS OF COOKIES

Refer to photos to decorate cookies.

First Day: Using First Day pattern (page 154), cut out shapes from Ginger Cookies dough (page 96); bake as directed. Pipe on pattern design with white Royal Icing (page 95). Add eyes.

Second Day: Prepare Chewy Caramel Turtles, this page.

Third Day: Using Third Day pattern (page 154), cut out shapes from Lemon Sugar Cookies dough (page 95); bake as directed. Tint Buttercream Frosting (page 95) with blue paste coloring; top with blue and white sprinkles. Add eyes.

Fourth Day: Using Fourth Day pattern (page 154), cut out shapes from Ginger Cookies dough (page 96); bake as directed. Tint half of Royal Icing (page 95) with red food coloring; leave remaining icing white. Ice half of cookies with red and remaining with white icing; let air-dry. Spoon remaining red and white icings into separate pastry bags fitted with small writing tip. Pipe on outlines in alternate color.

Fifth Day: Roll Lemon Sugar Cookies dough (page 95) into 1/2-inch-diameter ropes; cut 6 inches long. Brush ends with beaten egg; press ends together to form ring shape. Place on foil-lined baking sheets, spacing 1/2 inch apart. Brush lightly with beaten egg; sprinkle on coarse sugar crystals, pressing to adhere. Bake as directed.

Sixth Day: Using egg-shaped cookie cutter, cut out shapes from Ginger Cookies dough (page 96); bake as directed. Decorate with gold leaf.

Seventh Day: Prepare Meringue Cookies (page 97).

Eighth Day: Prepare Spotted-Cow Cookies (page 95).

Ninth Day: Using gingerbread-lady cookie cutter, cut out shapes from Ginger Cookies dough (page 96). Gently press pecans or almonds at bottom of cookies for feet. Bake as directed. Ice with Royal Icing (page 95) and decorate with silver dragées.

Note: Dragées are not recognized by the Food and Drug Administration as edible; use for decoration only.

Tenth Day: Using pattern (page 154), cut out shapes from Ginger Cookies dough (page 96). Bake as directed. Tint Royal Icing (page 95) with brown food coloring. Ice cutouts; let air-dry. Melt 3 ounces semisweet chocolate according to package directions. Place in plastic bag; squeeze chocolate into 1 corner and snip off tip of corner. Pipe chocolate onto pipes.

Eleventh Day: Using gingerbread-man cookie cutter, cut out shapes from Ginger Cookies dough (page 96); bake as directed. Dip feet in melted chocolate; let harden on waxed paper. Tint small amount of Buttercream Frosting (page 95) with red food coloring. Spoon into pastry bag fitted with basket-weave tip (or band tip). Pipe on red sashes.

Twelfth Day: Using Twelfth Day pattern (page 154), cut out shapes from Lemon Sugar Cookies dough (page 95); bake as directed. Divide Royal Icing (page 95) into fourths. Tint 1 batch red, 1 yellow and 1 blue; leave 1 white. Pipe icing onto cookies.

THE TWELVE DAYS OF cookies

Inspired by the beloved poem and carol "The Twelve Days of Christmas," our whimsical cookies and candy will fill the holiday season with fun for everyone. Shape these doughs as suggested, or cut and decorate them as you wish.

CHEWY CARAMEL TURTLES

- 2 cups pecan halves
- 1/2 pound soft caramels
- 2 teaspoons heavy cream
- 4 ounces German chocolate, chopped
- 2 ounces white chocolate, chopped

1. Spray baking sheet with nonstick vegetable-oil cooking spray. Arrange 5 pecan halves in turtle-shaped cluster on prepared baking sheet. Repeat with remaining pecans, making 24 clusters.

2. Place unwrapped caramels with cream in saucepan over very low heat, stirring constantly until caramels are melted; or microwave at full (100%) power for 3 minutes, stirring halfway during cooking time.

3. Spoon caramel mixture, by 1/2 rounded teaspoonfuls, into center of each nut cluster, slightly overlapping nuts. Let stand until set, about 30 minutes.

4. Place German chocolate in saucepan over very low heat, stirring constantly until melted; or microwave at full (100%) power for 2 minutes, stirring halfway during cooking time. Let cool slightly; spread over caramel mixture.

5. Place white chocolate in small saucepan over very low heat, stirring constantly until melted; or microwave at full (100%) power for 1 minute, stirring halfway through cooking time. Place in plastic bag and squeeze chocolate into 1 corner; snip off tip of corner. Pipe over German chocolate in a check pattern. Cool completely; store airtight, between sheets of waxed paper, in cool spot.
Yield: Makes 24 turtles.

ROYAL ICING

 4 tablespoons powdered egg whites
 4 tablespoons water
 2 cups confectioners' sugar
 1 tablespoon lemon juice
 Paste food colorings

In a bowl and using an electric mixer, beat egg whites and water until blended and foamy. Add sugar and lemon juice; beat at high speed until thickened and of good spreading consistency, about 2 minutes. Divide frosting and tint as you wish to decorate cookies.
Yield: Makes 3 to 4 cups.

BUTTERCREAM FROSTING

 $^1/_2$ cup (1 stick) butter or margarine, at room temperature
 1 box (1 pound) sifted confectioners' sugar
 3 to 4 tablespoons water
 Pinch salt
 Assorted food colorings

1. Cream butter in medium bowl; gradually beat in confectioners' sugar, salt and water until frosting is creamy smooth. Use as directed.
2. Divide into batches. Leave 1 batch frosting white; tint each of others with 1 or 2 drops other food colorings or as instructed in each cookie recipe.
3. Fit pastry bags with small plain tips. Fill with frostings; decorate as instructed in 12 Days of Cookies (page 94).

Yield: Makes enough to decorate sixty-four 3-inch cookies.

SPOTTED-COW COOKIES

 $2^1/_2$ cups all-purpose flour
 1 teaspoon baking powder
 $^1/_2$ teaspoon salt
 $^3/_4$ cup ($1^1/_2$ sticks) butter or margarine, at room temperature
 1 cup granulated sugar
 2 eggs
 1 teaspoon vanilla
 2 tablespoons unsweetened cocoa powder
 Coarse white decorative sugar

1. Prepare vanilla dough: Stir together $1^1/_4$ cups of flour, $^1/_2$ teaspoon baking powder and $^1/_4$ teaspoon salt in medium bowl.
2. Beat together 6 tablespoons butter, $^1/_2$ cup granulated sugar, 1 egg and $^1/_2$ teaspoon vanilla in large bowl until well blended. Gradually beat in flour mixture until dough forms. Shape dough into a flat disk. Wrap in plastic wrap; refrigerate several hours or overnight.
3. Prepare chocolate dough: Repeat Steps 1 and 2, adding cocoa powder to remaining flour, baking powder and salt.
4. Heat oven to 350°. Coat baking sheets with nonstick vegetable-oil cooking spray.
5. Roll vanilla dough out on lightly floured surface to $^3/_8$-inch thickness. Using 4 x 3-inch cow-shaped cookie cutter, cut out cows. With wide, flat metal spatula, transfer each cow to prepared baking sheet. Using $^3/_4$-inch round or scalloped cutter, cut 2 or 3 rounds from each cow; remove rounds to small baking sheet, and reserve for Step 7. Gather scraps of dough; shape into disk; wrap and refrigerate.
6. Repeat rolling and cutting with chocolate dough, refrigerating scraps.
7. Place vanilla rounds in cutouts on chocolate cows, and chocolate rounds on vanilla cows. If you wish to hang cookies, make hole in top center of each cow's back using straw or large plain round decorating tip.
8. Bake in 350° oven for 8 to 10 minutes or until lightly golden and crisp around

edges. Cool on sheet 1 minute. Remove to wire rack to cool.
9. Repeat rolling, cutting and baking until all scraps of dough have been used.
Yield: Makes $2^1/_2$ to 3 dozen cookies.

LEMON SUGAR COOKIES

 $2^1/_2$ cups all-purpose flour
 1 teaspoon baking powder
 $^1/_2$ teaspoon salt
 $^3/_4$ cup ($1^1/_2$ sticks) unsalted butter, softened
 1 cup sugar
 2 eggs
 1 tablespoon grated lemon zest
 1 tablespoon lemon juice

1. Combine flour, baking powder and salt in bowl.
2. Beat together butter, sugar and eggs in large bowl until well blended. Stir in lemon zest and juice. Stir in flour mixture until dough is smooth. Wrap dough in plastic wrap. Refrigerate several hours or overnight.
3. Heat oven to 400°. Divide dough in half. Roll out each half of dough on lightly floured surface to $^1/_8$-inch thickness. Cut out as directed for Third, Fifth or Twelfth Day cookies; or use any favorite 3- or 4-inch cookie cutters. Place $^1/_2$ inch apart on ungreased baking sheets.
4. Bake in 400° oven for 6 minutes or until lightly golden. Remove cookies to wire racks to cool. Decorate as directed, or as you wish.
Yield: Makes about forty 4-inch cookies.

GINGER COOKIES

  5 cups all-purpose flour
1½ tablespoons baking soda
  1 tablespoon ground ginger
  2 teaspoons ground cinnamon
½ teaspoon ground cloves
½ cup vegetable shortening
½ cup (1 stick) butter, softened
  1 cup firmly packed light-brown
     sugar
  1 egg
¾ cup molasses
  1 tablespoon distilled white vinegar

1. Sift together flour, baking soda, ginger, cinnamon and cloves in a small bowl.

2. In a large bowl and using an electric mixer on high speed, beat shortening and butter until creamy. Add brown sugar and egg; beat until fluffy. Add molasses and vinegar, beating just until combined.

3. Beat in 3 cups flour mixture on low speed until combined. Stir in remaining flour mixture with wooden spoon.

4. Divide dough into 4 equal parts. Shape each into a ball. Press to flatten slightly, then wrap in plastic wrap. Refrigerate dough until firm, 4 hours or overnight.

5. Heat oven to 375°. Lightly grease baking sheets.

6. Roll 1 ball dough on lightly floured surface to ⅛-inch thickness. Cut out as directed for First, Fourth, Sixth, Ninth, Tenth or Eleventh Day cookies; or use any favorite 3-inch cookie cutters. Place on lightly greased baking sheets.

7. Bake in 375° oven for 6 to 7 minutes or until lightly browned around edges. Remove cookies to wire racks to cool. Decorate as directed, or as you wish.

Yield: Makes about sixty-four 3-inch cookies.

*S*how your family how much you love them with a daily batch of Ginger Cookies (1, 4 and 6), Lemon Sugar Cookies (3 and 5) or Chewy Caramel Turtles (2).

On the first day of Christmas, my true love gave to me *1 partridge in a pear tree.*

On the second day of Christmas, my true love gave to me *2 turtle* doves.

On the third day of Christmas, my true love gave to me *3* French *hens.*

On the fourth day of Christmas, my true love gave to me *4 calling* birds.

On the fifth day of Christmas, my true love gave to me *5* golden *rings.*

On the sixth day of Christmas, my true love gave to me *6* geese *a-laying.*

On the seventh day of Christmas, my true love gave to me

7 *swans* a-swimming.

On the eighth day of Christmas, my true love gave to me

8 maids *a-milking*.

On the ninth day of Christmas, my true love gave to me

9 *ladies* dancing.

On the tenth day of Christmas, my true love gave to me

10 pipers *piping*.

On the eleventh day of Christmas, my true love gave to me

11 *lords* a-leaping.

On the twelfth day of Christmas, my true love gave to me

12 *drummers* drumming.

MERINGUE COOKIES

- $^3/_4$ cup sugar
- 3 egg whites
- $^1/_4$ teaspoon cream of tartar
  Pinch salt
- $^1/_4$ cup pecan pieces OR
  unblanched almond slivers

1. Line 2 baking sheets with aluminum foil. Coat foil very lightly with nonstick vegetable-oil cooking spray.
2. Place sugar in blender or food processor. Whirl for 2 minutes or until sugar is finely ground, scraping down sides as needed.
3. In a small bowl and using an electric mixer at medium speed, beat egg whites, cream of tartar, salt and 2 tablespoons ground sugar until frothy. Increase speed to high and beat egg white mixture until soft peaks form.
4. Beat in remaining sugar tablespoon by tablespoon; continue beating until stiff and glossy peaks form, about 5 minutes.
5. Spoon meringue into pastry bag fitted with medium star tip. Pipe meringues into 3-inch swans as pictured, this page. Place nut pieces on meringues for swans' beaks. Let meringues set for 30 minutes.
6. Heat oven to 200°.
7. Bake meringues in 200° oven for 2 hours or until firm. Let stand 10 minutes. Let cool to room temperature, then immediately place meringues in airtight containers until serving.
Note: You can recrisp meringues in 200° oven for 10 to 15 minutes.
Yield: Makes 20 meringues.

Shape light-as-air Meringue Cookies (7) with a pastry bag. Cocoa fans will want to eat Spotted-Cow Cookies (8) two-by-two! Ginger Cookies easily take a variety of shapes (9, 10 and 11). Lemon Sugar Cookies (12) get their zing from fruit juice and zest.

host a mix-and-mingle fete! Bring out our **tempting** lineup of festive **goodies** and an array of drinks. Finger foods allow guests to circulate easily, helping themselves to **tasty** morsels and good conversation. The best part? They're quick to fix, so you can have **fun** right along with your company!

BLACK BEAN DIP

1 tablespoon vegetable oil
1 medium-size onion, chopped
1 clove garlic, chopped
2 tablespoons water
½ ounce semisweet chocolate
1 can (19 ounces) black beans, drained and rinsed
1 can (4 ounces) chopped green chilies, drained
½ teaspoon salt
3 avocados
½ medium-size red onion, diced
1½ tablespoons fresh lemon juice
1 cup shredded Cheddar cheese (4 ounces)
1 tomato, seeded and diced
½ cup sour cream
2 green onions, sliced diagonally
Tortilla chips (optional)

1. Heat oil in medium-size skillet over medium heat. Add chopped onion and garlic; sauté for 6 minutes or until softened. Add water and chocolate; cook 1 to 2 minutes or until chocolate melts. Place onion mixture, black beans, chilies and salt in food processor or blender. Whirl until puréed. Pour onto round shallow serving platter.
2. Peel and seed avocados. Scoop flesh into a medium-size bowl. Add red onion and lemon juice; mash together with fork. Carefully spread evenly over top of bean mixture, leaving an edge showing.
3. Sprinkle Cheddar cheese over top of avocado mixture. Mound tomato on top. Dollop with sour cream. Garnish with green onions. Serve with tortilla chips, if desired.
Yield: Makes 16 servings.

*U*se your favorite mini-ravioli — fresh or frozen — for pop-in-your-mouth Ravioli Crisps With Basil Dipping Sauce (above). They'll be appreciated by kids and grown-ups alike. Spicy Black Bean Dip (opposite), heaped with avocado and Cheddar, has a surprisingly scrumptious secret ingredient!

RAVIOLI CRISPS WITH BASIL DIPPING SAUCE

4 cups vegetable oil
1 box (16 ounces, 48-count) small cheese ravioli, fresh or frozen, thawed and patted dry
2 cups marinara sauce, homemade or bottled
2 tablespoons chopped fresh basil

1. Fill medium-size saucepan with oil, making sure there is at least 6 inches between top of oil and top of pan. Heat oil over medium heat until oil registers 300° on deep-fry thermometer. Line baking sheet with paper towels.
2. With metal slotted spoon, carefully add 8 ravioli at a time to hot oil to avoid overcrowding; fry for 1 to 2 minutes or until ravioli turn light brown. Adjust heat as needed to maintain temperature. With slotted spoon, remove ravioli to prepared baking sheet to drain.
3. Heat together marinara sauce and basil in small saucepan for 2 to 3 minutes or until hot. Pour into small serving dish. Serve alongside ravioli.
Note: Ravioli can be fried up to 2 hours ahead. To serve, place on a baking sheet and reheat in a 400° oven for 5 to 10 minutes or until hot.
Yield: Makes 48 ravioli.

PEPPERONI FRENCH BREAD PIZZA

- 1 loaf Italian bread (about 12 ounces), split in half horizontally
- 1¼ cups bottled pasta sauce
- 4 ounces raw mushrooms, thinly sliced
- 1 ounce pepperoni, finely chopped
- 1 cup coarsely shredded part-skim mozzarella (4 ounces)
- 1 teaspoon dried oregano
  Pinch each of salt and ground black pepper
- 2 tablespoons grated Parmesan cheese

1. Heat oven to 400°. Place bread halves, cut side up, on baking sheet. Pull out some of soft bread centers to make loaves slightly concave. Spread each half with ½ cup of pasta sauce. Arrange mushrooms over sauce; sprinkle with pepperoni. Top with mozzarella; sprinkle with oregano, salt and pepper. Spoon remaining pasta sauce over tops.
2. Bake in 400° oven until lightly browned, about 15 minutes. Sprinkle with Parmesan. Cut on angle into slices. Serve hot.
Yield: Makes 8 servings.

MARINATED OLIVES

- 1 cup olives
- ½ cup olive oil

Flavorings:
- 2 teaspoons grated orange zest and 1 teaspoon fennel seed OR
- 2 teaspoons grated lemon zest, ½ teaspoon red-pepper flakes, ½ teaspoon cumin seed and 1 teaspoon crushed black pepper OR
- 2 cloves garlic, chopped, and 1 teaspoon chopped fresh rosemary

Mix olives and oil in glass jar. Add desired flavorings. Cover and marinate in refrigerator at least 48 hours, up to a month.
Yield: Makes 1¼ cups.

Serve savory temptations with a minimum of last-minute fuss. Speedy Pepperoni French Bread Pizza (above) will please guests of all ages. Season a variety of Marinated Olives (opposite, left) with your pick of Mediterranean flavors: fennel, cumin, red pepper, garlic and rosemary — guaranteed to be an instant party hit!

POTTED SPINACH SPREAD
Prepare ahead, pack into a crock and chill.

- 1 pound fresh spinach, stemmed and rinsed
- 1 package (8 ounces) cream cheese, at room temperature
- $^1/_2$ cup sour cream
- $^1/_2$ teaspoon dried tarragon or basil
- $^1/_2$ teaspoon grated nutmeg
- $^1/_2$ teaspoon salt
- $^1/_2$ teaspoon ground black pepper
- $^1/_2$ cup chopped pimiento
- Pimiento, for garnish
- Whole-wheat crackers and sliced vegetables, for dipping

1. Cook wet spinach leaves in large nonreactive pot, covered, over high heat until wilted, about 3 minutes; stir once or twice. Drain; let cool in sieve. Squeeze out excess liquid. Chop spinach; you should have about 1 cup.
2. Purée spinach and cream cheese in food processor. Add sour cream, tarragon, nutmeg, salt and pepper; blend to combine. Stir in pimiento. Pack into crock or bowl. Chill overnight. Garnish top with triangles of pimiento. Serve with crackers and sliced vegetables.
Yield: Makes about 2$^1/_2$ cups.

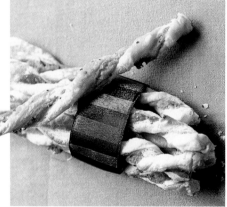

Frozen puff pastry takes the work out of Rosemary Cheese Straws. Serve plenty of crackers and fresh veggies with the creamy Potted Spinach Spread (not shown).

ROSEMARY CHEESE STRAWS
Try other fresh herbs such as marjoram or oregano.

- $^1/_2$ cup grated Parmesan cheese
- 2 tablespoons butter, melted
- 1 teaspoon chopped fresh rosemary
- $^1/_2$ teaspoon ground black pepper
- $^1/_2$ of 17.3-ounce package frozen puff pastry (1 sheet), thawed following package directions
- 1 egg
- 1 tablespoon water

1. Heat oven to 400°. Lightly butter 2 large baking sheets.
2. Stir together cheese, butter, rosemary and pepper in bowl.
3. Unfold pastry on floured surface. Roll into a 14 x 10-inch rectangle. Halve lengthwise. Spread half with cheese mixture. Top with remaining rectangle. Roll with rolling pin to seal.
4. Cut across width into twenty-eight $^1/_2$-inch strips. Twist strips; place 1 inch apart on prepared baking sheets, pressing down ends to attach to baking sheet. Stir egg and water in small bowl. Brush twists lightly with egg wash.
5. Bake in 400° oven for 10 minutes. Lower to 300°. Bake until deep golden and very crispy, 15 to 20 minutes. Cool on racks. Store in airtight container up to 2 weeks.
Yield: Makes 28 straws.

Pineapple gives a juicy burst to Sesame Shrimp Skewers (opposite). *For a peppery contrast, offer Sweet Spicy Chicken Skewers as well. Keep the occasion merry with a sampler of warm Savory Scones* (right) *in a medley of flavors: Ham and Sage, Cheddar Cheese and Rosemary and Black Olive.*

SESAME SHRIMP SKEWERS

- 1 can (8 ounces) pineapple chunks, packed in juice
- $1/3$ cup low-sodium soy sauce
- 2 tablespoons sugar
- 1 tablespoon rice-wine vinegar
- 1 tablespoon plum wine OR sherry
- 2 quarter-size pieces peeled fresh ginger
- 1 green onion, finely chopped
- 1 teaspoon dark Asian sesame oil
- 1 pound large shrimp (about 24), peeled and deveined
- 1 pint cherry tomatoes (about 24)

1. Drain canned pineapple, reserving juice.
2. Combine soy sauce, sugar, vinegar, plum wine, fresh ginger, green onion and oil in a blender or food processor. Whirl until puréed. Transfer marinade to plastic food storage bag. Add the reserved pineapple juice. Add shrimp; seal and turn bag to coat shrimp. Refrigerate for 1 hour.
3. Soak 8 small wooden skewers in water for 15 minutes to prevent scorching during cooking.
4. Heat broiler. Thread shrimp, tomatoes and pineapple on skewers. Place skewers on rack in broiler pan; spoon some marinade over skewers.
5. Broil 3 inches from heat for about 6 minutes or until shrimp are cooked through, turning once and basting again with marinade.
Yield: Makes 8 skewers.

SWEET SPICY CHICKEN SKEWERS

- 1 can (4 ounces) green chilies, drained
- 1 green onion, cut in 1-inch pieces
- 2 cloves garlic
- $1/4$ cup bottled plum sauce or jam
- 1 tablespoon soy sauce
- 1 teaspoon dark Asian sesame oil
- $1/2$ teaspoon salt
- 2 skinless, boneless chicken breast halves (about 4 ounces each), cut into $1^1/2$-inch cubes
- 1 sweet green pepper, cored, seeded and cut into 1-inch-square pieces
- 1 medium-size onion, cut into 1-inch pieces
- 1 sweet red pepper, cored, seeded and cut into 1-inch-square pieces

1. Combine drained chilies, green onion, garlic, plum sauce, soy sauce, sesame oil and salt in a food processor or blender. Whirl until puréed.
2. Place chicken in a medium-size bowl. Add half of plum sauce mixture. Cover; refrigerate for 1 hour to marinate. Reserve remaining half of plum mixture.
3. Soak 16 small wooden skewers in water for 15 minutes to prevent scorching during cooking.
4. Heat broiler. Thread green pepper, onion, red pepper and chicken cubes on skewers. Place skewers on rack in broiler pan. Spoon on remaining reserved plum mixture over skewers.
5. Broil 6 inches from heat for 6 to 8 minutes or until chicken is cooked through, turning once.
Yield: Makes 16 skewers.

SAVORY SCONES

- $2^3/4$ cups all-purpose flour
- 4 teaspoons baking powder
- $3/4$ teaspoon salt
- $1/4$ teaspoon baking soda
- $1/2$ cup (1 stick) unsalted butter, cut into 16 pieces
- 1 to $1^1/4$ cups buttermilk

1. Heat oven to 400°.

2. Combine flour, baking powder, salt and baking soda in food processor. Pulse once or twice to combine. Add butter. Pulse 10 to 12 times or until mixture resembles fresh bread crumbs. (The butter can also be cut into flour using a pastry blender or your fingertips.)

3. Transfer mixture to a large bowl. Add 1 cup buttermilk, stirring quickly to combine. If mixture is too dry, add more buttermilk, 1 tablespoon at a time, until dough holds together and is slightly stringy and crumbly. Turn out onto a lightly floured surface. Knead 6 to 7 times (do not knead more than that or scones will become tough).

4. Divide dough in half. With floured hands, press each half into a 9 x 4-inch rectangle. With a short side facing you, fold into thirds like a business letter. Press each portion into a 6- to 7-inch circle; place on ungreased baking sheet. Cut each circle into 6 equal wedges; pull wedges slightly apart. Brush tops with remaining buttermilk. Let stand 10 minutes.

5. Bake in 400° oven for 20 minutes or until tops are lightly browned. Remove and serve warm.

Yield: Makes 12 scones.

Ham and Sage Scones: Add 4 ounces cubed boiled ham and 1 teaspoon dried sage along with butter. Pulse 10 to 12 times until ham pieces are no larger than grains of rice. Instead of pressing dough into circles, press each half into a 7½-inch square. Cut each into 8 squares.

Yield: Makes 16 scones.

Cheddar Cheese Scones: Add 4 ounces cubed Cheddar and ¼ to ½ teaspoon cayenne pepper along with butter. Process 10 to 12 times until cheese pieces are no larger than dried peas. After brushing tops with buttermilk, sprinkle with sesame seeds, using about 2 teaspoons total.

Yield: Makes 12 scones.

Rosemary and Black Olive Scones: After dividing dough in half, scatter ½ teaspoon crumbled dried rosemary and ¼ cup chopped kalamata olives (about 10 olives) over each batch of dough before it is folded into thirds.

Yield: Makes 12 scones.

PESTO CHEESE FOR VEGETABLES

1½ cups low-fat (1%) cottage cheese
½ cup part-skim ricotta cheese (50% less fat)
2 tablespoons light cream cheese (50% less fat)
1 tablespoon grated Parmesan cheese
2 teaspoons fresh lemon juice
1 cup packed fresh basil leaves
1 green onion, chopped
1 clove garlic, finely chopped
   Assorted cut-up vegetables, for dipping

1. Combine cottage cheese, ricotta, cream cheese, Parmesan and lemon juice in food processor or blender. Whirl until almost smooth.

2. Add basil, green onion and garlic. Pulse with on-off motion until mixture is finely chopped.

3. Serve at once or cover and refrigerate up to 3 days.

Yield: Makes 3 cups.

CHRISTMAS SANGRIA

4 navel oranges, sliced
2 lemons, sliced
1½ cups sugar
2 bottles (750 ml each) dry white wine, chilled
1 can (12 ounces) frozen cranberry juice cocktail concentrate, thawed
2 tablespoons orange-flavored liqueur
2 tablespoons brandy
1 bottle (1 liter) club soda, chilled

1. Place fruit slices in a large bowl. Pour sugar over fruit; stir with a wooden spoon until fruit is coated with sugar. Cover and let stand at room temperature 1 hour.

2. In a large container, combine fruit mixture, wine, cranberry juice concentrate, liqueur and brandy. Cover and chill 2 hours.

3. To serve: Transfer wine mixture to a 5-quart serving container; stir in club soda. Serve immediately.

Yield: Makes about 14 cups wine.

Flavorful Pesto Cheese (opposite) is a great go-with for heaps of cut-up veggies, while Christmas Sangria (not shown) sparkles with holiday cheer. The taste is as rich as ever, but our festive Eggnog (below) uses whipped frozen evaporated skim milk in place of heavy cream. Vanilla ice cream and brown sugar sweeten the spirited Praline Coffee (not shown).

EGGNOG

3 eggs
3 egg whites
³/₄ cup sugar
¹/₄ teaspoon salt
4 cups low-fat milk
¹/₂ cup brandy (optional)
1 tablespoon vanilla
¹/₂ teaspoon ground nutmeg
1 can (12 ounces) evaporated skim milk
  Nutmeg and cinnamon sticks, for garnish

1. Whisk eggs, whites, sugar and salt in 2-quart saucepan. Gradually stir in low-fat milk. Cook over low heat, stirring, until mixture thickens and coats back of spoon, about 25 minutes (should register 170° to 175° on instant-read thermometer); do not let boil. Pour into bowl. Stir in brandy, if using, vanilla and nutmeg. Chill 3 hours.
2. Pour skim milk into ice-cube tray. Freeze 2 hours or until almost frozen. Empty cubes into metal bowl. Beat at medium speed until soft peaks form, 10 minutes. Gently fold into custard mixture. Pour into chilled punch bowl. Sprinkle with nutmeg and serve with cinnamon stick.
Yield: Makes 16 servings.

PRALINE COFFEE

2 quarts brewed coffee
3 cans (12 ounces each) evaporated skim milk
¹/₂ cup firmly packed brown sugar
3 cups fat-free vanilla ice cream, softened
1 cup vodka
1 tablespoon vanilla
2 teaspoons maple flavoring

1. In a Dutch oven, combine coffee, evaporated milk and brown sugar. Stirring occasionally, cook over medium-high heat until mixture begins to boil; remove from heat.
2. Stir in ice cream, vodka, vanilla and maple flavoring. Serve hot.
Yield: Makes about twenty 6-ounce servings.

Sweet
SENSATIONS

MANGO MOUSSE CAKE

1 prepared pound cake (about 12 ounces), thawed if frozen
²/₃ cup raspberry jam
3 envelopes unflavored gelatin
¹/₂ cup plus 6 tablespoons water
2 mangoes, pitted, peeled and diced
3 tablespoons orange liqueur
1 teaspoon grated fresh ginger
³/₄ cup sugar
2 tablespoons powdered egg whites
1 cup heavy cream, whipped

1. Trim crust off cake. From bottom, horizontally cut four ¹/₂-inch-thick slices. Spread each with 2 tablespoons jam; stack. Cut in half lengthwise, then crosswise into eighths.
2. Grease 9-inch springform pan. Arrange cake stacks against side of pan around base; stand on edge so jam lines are vertical; place stacks, jam edge to plain edge. Crumble remaining cake into center. Using waxed paper, press firmly in even layer. Remove paper; gently spread remaining jam over cake layer. Refrigerate. (Can be made 2 days ahead.)
3. Soften gelatin in ¹/₂ cup water in small saucepan, 5 minutes. Heat, stirring, until gelatin has dissolved.
4. Purée mango, liqueur, ginger and ¹/₄ cup sugar in processor. Transfer to bowl; add gelatin. Chill, stirring often, until thick like egg whites.
5. Beat powdered egg whites and 6 tablespoons water in bowl to form soft peaks. Gradually beat in remaining sugar to form stiff peaks. Fold into mango mixture. Fold in whipped cream. Pour into prepared pan. Chill 5 hours or overnight to set.
Yield: Makes 12 servings.

Heavenly Mango Mousse Cake (opposite) starts with a purchased pound cake — but no one has to know! The cranberry filling of our Sour Cream Pistachio Pie (right) covers a store-bought crust and strikes a perfect balance between sweet and tart.

SOUR CREAM PISTACHIO PIE

1 bag (12 ounces) fresh or frozen cranberries, coarsely chopped
1³/₄ cups sugar
1 ready-to-use refrigerated piecrust for single-crust 9-inch pie
1 egg, lightly beaten
2 tablespoons cornstarch
²/₃ cup coarsely chopped pistachios
1 apple, peeled, cored and diced
1 container (8 ounces) sour cream
Vanilla ice cream (optional)

1. Mix cranberries and 1 cup sugar in saucepan. Cover; cook, stirring occasionally, over medium-high heat 20 minutes or until thick and berries pop. Let cool.
2. Heat oven to 400°. Roll out piecrust to fit 9-inch pie plate. Transfer into plate; flute edge. Prick crust with fork. Line with aluminum foil; fill with dried beans.
3. Bake in 400° oven for 10 minutes. Remove foil and weights. Brush crust with egg.
4. Whisk remaining ³/₄ cup sugar and cornstarch in large bowl. Add pistachios, apple and sour cream. Add cooked cranberries. Pour into crust. Place plate on baking sheet for drips.
5. Bake in 400° oven for 50 minutes or until bubbly. After first 20 minutes, cover edges of crust with foil to prevent overbrowning. Cool on rack. Serve with ice cream, if you wish.
Yield: Makes 12 servings.

bring any **festivity** to a close on the happiest of notes — pick one confection or a sampling of our **scrumptious** specialties as a sweet, sensational ending to your Yuletide **celebration**.

MINI FIG BUNDT CAKES

Cakes:

- 1 package (8 ounces) dried figs
- 1¼ cups all-purpose flour
- ¾ teaspoon baking powder
- ½ teaspoon baking soda
- ¼ teaspoon salt
    Pinch ground cloves
    Pinch ground cinnamon
- 6 tablespoons (¾ stick) butter, at room temperature
- ¾ cup packed dark-brown sugar
- 2 eggs
- 1 teaspoon vanilla
- ⅔ cup sour cream
- ¼ cup milk
- ¼ cup chopped walnuts
- 1 teaspoon grated orange zest

Glaze:

- ¾ cup confectioners' sugar
- 1 tablespoon milk
    Strips of orange zest, for garnish (optional)

1. Prepare Cakes: Mix 8 figs and 3 tablespoons hot water in processor or blender. Purée until smooth. Chop remaining figs (should have about ½ cup chopped).

2. Heat oven to 350°. Grease six 1-cup mini Bundt cake molds or one 12-cup Bundt pan (see Note).

3. Sift together flour, baking powder, baking soda, salt, cloves and cinnamon into a bowl.

4. Beat butter in another bowl until smooth, 2 minutes. Add brown sugar; beat until light and fluffy, 2 minutes. Add eggs, one at a time, beating well after each. Beat in vanilla.

5. Mix puréed figs, sour cream and milk in small bowl. On low speed, beat flour mixture into butter mixture in 3 additions, alternating with fig mixture, beginning and ending with flour. Fold in chopped figs, walnuts and orange zest. Divide into Bundt molds.

6. Bake in 350° oven for 20 to 22 minutes or until cakes spring back when lightly touched. Transfer pan to rack and cool 10 minutes. Invert pan onto rack, tapping bottom to release cakes. Cool cakes.

7. Prepare Glaze: Beat confectioners' sugar and milk in small bowl until good glazing consistency. Drizzle glaze over cooled cakes. Garnish with strips of orange zest, if you wish.

Yield: Makes 6 mini cakes or 1 large cake.

Note: For 12-cup Bundt pan, double recipe for cakes and glaze. Bake at 350° for 55 to 60 minutes.

Mini Fig Bundt Cakes are diminutive delights full of figs and walnuts. Pair with a hot cup of coffee for a snack that seems especially right for the season.

MOCHA FUDGE CUPS

Everyone will love Mocha Fudge Cups. Rich with butter and marshmallow creme, they're "iced" with purchased candy decorations.

1   jar (7½ ounces) marshmallow creme
1   cup sugar
⅔   cup evaporated milk
¼   cup (½ stick) unsalted butter
3   tablespoons instant-coffee powder or crystals
¼   teaspoon salt
1   package (12 ounces) semisweet chocolate chips
      Purchased candy decorations

1. Arrange 1¼-inch foil or paper candy cups in shallow pan. Spray lightly with nonstick vegetable-oil cooking spray.
2. Combine marshmallow creme, sugar, evaporated milk, butter, coffee powder and salt in heavy medium saucepan. Bring to full boil; boil 5 minutes over medium heat, stirring constantly. Remove from heat.
3. Add chocolate chips, stirring constantly, until chocolate is melted and smooth. Spoon into cups; gently place candy decorations on top.
4. Chill at least 2 hours or until firm. Store in refrigerator in airtight containers up to 2 weeks.
Yield: Makes 70 pieces.

Partygoers will love these dazzling do-ahead treats. Linzer Torte (top) mixes the crunch of nuts with the sweet goodness of raspberry jam. In our Lemony Fruit Tart (bottom), the unique flavors of fresh kiwis and tangy lemon curd blend together for stunning results.

LINZER TORTE

3	cups all-purpose flour
1½	teaspoons ground cinnamon
1	teaspoon salt
1¼	cups (2½ sticks) butter, cut into pieces
1½	cups sugar
1	pound walnuts, finely ground
1	egg, slightly beaten
1	egg yolk, slightly beaten
2	jars (12 ounces each) seedless raspberry jam
1	egg yolk
1	teaspoon water
⅓	cup slivered almonds

1. Place oven rack in lower third of oven. Heat oven to 400°.

2. Combine flour, cinnamon and salt in bowl. Cut in butter with pastry blender until mixture resembles coarse crumbs. Stir in sugar and walnuts. Stir in whole egg and yolk. Work into large ball; halve.

3. Coat a 15½ x 10½ x 1-inch jelly-roll pan with nonstick vegetable-oil cooking spray. Press half of dough into pan and up sides.

4. Bake in 400° oven for 12 to 15 minutes or until barely colored.

5. Meanwhile, roll remaining dough between sheets of waxed paper to ¼-inch thickness. Put on baking sheet in freezer 15 minutes.

6. Reduce oven temperature to 350°. Reset rack in upper third of oven.

7. Spread jam over baked tart bottom. Remove top piece of waxed paper from chilled dough. Cut into ½- to ¾-inch-wide diagonal strips. Arrange in lattice pattern on top of jelly, ½ to ¾ inch apart, piecing strips, if necessary. Press ends of strips to edge. Place strips around edge for border; score strips, with fork.

8. Mix yolk and water. Brush over pastry. Decorate edge with almonds.

9. Bake in 350° oven for 35 minutes or until browned. Cool on rack.

Yield: Makes 24 servings.

LEMONY FRUIT TART

Crust:

1½	cups all-purpose flour
½	teaspoon salt
⅓	cup butter, chilled and cut into pieces
¼	cup solid vegetable shortening
4	to 5 tablespoons ice water

Filling:

¾	cup heavy cream
3	tablespoons confectioners' sugar
2	tablespoons bottled lemon curd
1	teaspoon grated lemon zest

Fruit:

4	kiwifruit, peeled and thinly sliced into rounds
8	red grapes
¼	cup pasteurized egg white
1	tablespoon sugar

1. Prepare Crust: Stir together flour and salt in medium-size bowl. With pastry blender, cut in butter and shortening until mixture is crumbly. Drizzle ice water over mixture, tossing with fork, until dough begins to hold together when pressed. Gather dough into ball. Wrap in plastic wrap; press into disk; refrigerate 30 minutes.

2. Heat oven to 450°.

3. Between 2 sheets of plastic wrap, roll out dough to fit pan: For rectangular 11 x 7-inch pan, roll into 13 x 8½-inch rectangle; for 9-inch round tart pan with removable bottom, roll into 11-inch circle. Transfer pastry to pan, discarding wrap, and patching to fit, if necessary. Prick crust lightly all over with fork. Line pastry with foil; fill with dried beans or pie weights.

4. Bake in 450° oven for 8 minutes. Remove foil and weights. Bake for another 8 to 10 minutes or until crust is golden. Remove pan to a wire rack to cool completely.

5. Prepare Filling: Beat heavy cream with confectioners' sugar in medium-size bowl until stiff peaks form. Fold in lemon curd and lemon zest. Spread filling evenly over bottom of cooled pastry crust.

6. Prepare Fruit: Layer on kiwi slices, overlapping slightly. Dip grapes into egg white, letting excess drip off. Dip into sugar; place decoratively on top of tart. Serve slightly chilled or at room temperature.

Yield: Makes 8 servings.

LEMON-POPPY SEED CAKE

2^1/$_2$	cups unsifted all-purpose flour
1^1/$_4$	teaspoons baking powder
1	teaspoon baking soda
^{3}/$_4$	teaspoon salt
^{2}/$_3$	cup unsalted butter or margarine, at room temperature
1	cup sugar
3	eggs
1	cup buttermilk
^{1}/$_3$	cup poppy seeds
1	tablespoon grated lemon zest
4	egg whites
	Lemon Glaze (recipe follows)
	Sugared Lemon Zest and Sugared Strawberries (optional; recipe follows)

1. Heat oven to 325°. Grease and flour 12-cup (10-inch) tube or Bundt pan.
2. Combine flour, baking powder, baking soda and salt in bowl.
3. Beat together butter and ^{3}/$_4$ cup sugar in large bowl until light and fluffy. Beat in 3 eggs, one at a time.
4. Add flour mixture alternately with buttermilk to egg mixture, starting and ending with dry ingredients and beating well after each addition; beat until smooth. Beat in poppy seeds and lemon zest.
5. Beat remaining 4 egg whites in large bowl until foamy. Gradually beat in remaining ^{1}/$_4$ cup sugar until soft peaks form. Fold into batter until no white remains. Pour into prepared pan.
6. Bake in 325° oven for 45 to 50 minutes or until top springs back when lightly touched with finger. Let stand 15 minutes. Loosen cake around

tube and sides with spatula; invert onto rack to cool completely. Spoon or drizzle Lemon Glaze over top of cake, letting it drip down sides. Garnish with lemon zest and strawberries, if you wish.

Yield: Makes 14 servings.

Lemon Glaze: Whisk together 2 cups confectioners' sugar, 2 tablespoons milk, 2 teaspoons grated lemon zest, 1^1/$_2$ teaspoons fresh lemon juice and ^{1}/$_8$ teaspoon salt in bowl until well blended and smooth. To thin glaze for drizzle, stir in additional milk, drop by drop, until drizzling consistency.

Sugared Lemon Zest and Sugared Strawberries: Remove lemon zest with swivel-bladed vegetable peeler; cut into very thin strips. Lightly brush zest and strawberries with maple syrup. Lightly sprinkle with granulated sugar.

Sometimes it's the simple goodness of an easy snack cake that holiday munchers crave most. Lemon-Poppy Seed Cake offers slices of fruit-flavored sweetness — a just-right companion for a cup of tea.

*O*ur gorgeous Grasshopper Pie (below), spiked with crème de menthe and crème de cocoa, nestles in a chocolate-crumb crust. For Christmastime or anytime, you can bake several small Cranberry-Pear Tarts (opposite). Top the gingery filling with sugar-dusted stars you cut from the hazelnut crust.

GRASSHOPPER PIE

Crust:
- 1⅓ cups chocolate-cookie crumbs
- ¼ cup granulated sugar
- 6 tablespoons butter, melted

Filling:
- 4 squares (1 ounce each) white baking chocolate, chopped
- 4 tablespoons crème de menthe
- 1 tablespoon crème de cocoa
- 6 ounces cream cheese, at room temperature
- ¼ cup confectioners' sugar
- 1½ cups heavy cream, whipped Chocolate Curls (recipe follows), fresh mint sprigs and fresh raspberries, for garnish

1. Heat oven to 375°. Spray 9-inch removable-bottom tart pan lightly with nonstick vegetable-oil cooking spray.
2. Prepare Crust: Combine crumbs, granulated sugar and butter in bowl until blended. Press mixture into prepared pan, patting crumbs in even layer on bottom and up sides of pan. Bake in 375° oven for 7 minutes; cool crust completely on wire rack.
3. Prepare Filling: Combine chocolate and 2 tablespoons of the crème de menthe in small saucepan. Cook over lowest heat, stirring constantly, just until chocolate is melted. Remove from heat; stir in remaining crème de menthe and the crème de cocoa.
4. Beat cream cheese and confectioners' sugar with electric mixer until smooth. Beat in chocolate mixture until combined. Fold in whipped cream. Spoon mixture into cooled crust, swirling top decoratively with back of spoon. Cover loosely with plastic and refrigerate 1 hour or until ready to serve. Decorate with Chocolate Curls, mint and raspberries.
Yield: Makes 10 servings.
Chocolate Curls: Line 2 large baking sheets with waxed paper. Line an 8½ x 4½ x 2-inch loaf pan with aluminum foil. Melt one 12-ounce package semisweet- or milk-chocolate morsels with 1 tablespoon vegetable shortening until smooth. Pour into prepared loaf pan. Refrigerate 1 hour or just until firm in center (if too firm, chocolate will not curl). Use cheese slicer

to form curls. Or turn out chocolate onto board; cut in half lengthwise, then crosswise into 4 bars the width of a swivel-bladed vegetable peeler. Scrape peeler down bars. Lift curls off blade with wooden pick; set on prepared baking sheets. Refrigerate at least 30 minutes before using. If bars soften, chill until firm enough to handle. Spray blade as needed with nonstick vegetable-oil cooking spray to prevent sticking.

CRANBERRY-PEAR TARTS

Crust:
- 1 cup sugar
- ¾ cup toasted hazelnuts, skinned (see Note)
- 2 cups all-purpose flour
- ½ teaspoon baking powder
- ¾ teaspoon ground cinnamon
- ¼ teaspoon salt
- ¾ cup (1½ sticks) unsalted butter, cut into pieces
- 1 egg
- 1 tablespoon heavy cream or milk

Filling:
- 1 cup sugar
- 2 tablespoons cornstarch
- 2 cups (8 ounces) fresh or frozen cranberries
- 2 pears (1 pound) peeled, cored and diced
- 2 tablespoons honey
- 2 teaspoons freshly grated gingerroot

- ¼ teaspoon ground allspice Confectioners' sugar (optional)

1. Prepare Crust: Combine sugar and toasted hazelnuts in food processor. Process 1 minute or until nuts are finely ground. Add flour, baking powder, cinnamon, salt and butter. Process 1 minute or until blended. Add egg and cream; process, using on-off pulses, until mixture is combined and starts to come together. Set aside 2 cups of mixture for tart shells; flatten remaining dough into a disk. Wrap in plastic, chill and reserve for star cutouts.
2. Heat oven to 375°. Spray eight 4-inch-diameter removable-bottom tart pans and a small baking sheet with nonstick vegetable-oil cooking spray. Using floured hands, pat ¼ cup tart-shell mixture to even thickness in bottom and ¾ inch up sides of each tart pan. Repeat with remaining dough. Chill 30 minutes.
3. Meanwhile, roll remaining dough to ⅛-inch thickness in between sheets of lightly floured waxed paper. Cut out stars, using ½-inch, 1½-inch and 3-inch star-shaped cookie cutters. Place on prepared baking sheet.
4. Bake stars in 375° oven for 6 to 8 minutes or until lightly golden. Remove from baking sheet and let cool on wire rack.
5. Bake tart shells in 375° oven for 12 to 14 minutes or until lightly golden. Transfer to rack to cool for 5 minutes. Remove tart shells from pans.
6. Prepare Filling: Stir together sugar and cornstarch in medium saucepan. Stir in cranberries, pears, honey, ginger and allspice. Bring to a simmer; stir occasionally for 8 minutes or until thickened. Remove from heat; cool.
7. Spoon cooled filling into prepared shells, dividing evenly (rounded ⅓ cup filling per shell). Arrange stars on top of tarts, dusting lightly with confectioners' sugar, if you wish.
Yield: Makes 8 servings.
Note: To toast hazelnuts, heat oven to 350°. Spread hazelnuts on baking sheet and bake in 350° oven for 10 to 15 minutes or until toasted. Rub hazelnuts in clean kitchen towel to remove skins.

CRAN-NUT MINI BUNDT CAKES

1¼ cups all-purpose flour
¾ teaspoon baking powder
½ teaspoon baking soda
¼ teaspoon salt
6 tablespoons (¾ stick) butter or
  margarine, at room temperature
¾ cup sugar
1 teaspoon vanilla
2 eggs
⅔ cup sour cream
½ cup dried cranberries, chopped
¼ cup pecans, chopped
  Confectioners' sugar for dusting
  Sweetened, cooked cranberries,
  for garnish (optional)

1. Heat oven to 350°. Coat six 1-cup mini Bundt cake molds with nonstick vegetable-oil cooking spray.
2. Mix flour, baking powder, baking soda and salt in bowl.
3. Beat butter, sugar and vanilla in another bowl until fluffy. Beat in eggs, one at a time. Stir in flour mixture alternately with sour cream, just to moisten. Fold in cranberries and pecans. Divide into prepared molds.
4. Bake in 350° oven for 20 to 23 minutes or until wooden pick inserted near center comes out clean. Unmold onto wire racks to cool. Dust with confectioners' sugar. Fill centers with cooked cranberries, if you wish.
Yield: Makes 6 mini cakes.

COOKIES-AND-CREAM CUPCAKES

Cupcakes:
1¾ cups all-purpose flour
2 teaspoons baking powder
½ teaspoon salt
⅓ cup butter or margarine, at
  room temperature
¾ cup sugar
1 egg
¾ cup milk
1 tablespoon grated orange zest
1 teaspoon vanilla
5 chocolate sandwich cookies,
  coarsely broken up

Creamy Chocolate Frosting:
½ cup heavy cream

¼ cup presweetened chocolate
  drink mix
  Broken chocolate sandwich
  cookies, for garnish (optional)

1. Place oven rack in lower third of oven. Heat oven to 375°. Coat cupcake-pan cups with nonstick vegetable-oil cooking spray or insert paper liners.
2. Prepare Cupcakes: Mix flour, baking powder and salt in bowl.
3. Beat butter and sugar in another bowl until creamy. Add egg; beat well. Alternately beat in milk with flour mixture, beginning and ending with flour, until smooth. Beat in zest and vanilla. Stir in cookie pieces.
4. Spoon batter into prepared cups, filling each about two-thirds full.
5. Bake in lower third of 375° oven for 14 minutes or until wooden pick inserted in centers comes out clean and tops spring back when lightly touched. Cool in pan on rack 5 minutes. Gently loosen cupcakes from pan; remove to rack to cool.
6. Prepare Creamy Chocolate Frosting: Beat together cream and drink mix in small bowl until soft peaks form. Spread over top of cupcakes. Garnish with broken cookies, if you wish.
Yield: Makes 12 cupcakes.

RASPBERRY CRUMB BARS

2 cups all-purpose flour
1 teaspoon baking powder
½ teaspoon salt
1 cup almonds (about 4 ounces)
¾ cup (1½ sticks) butter, at
  room temperature
1 teaspoon vanilla
⅔ cup sugar
1 egg
1 jar (12 ounces) raspberry
  preserves

1. Heat oven to 375°. Coat a 13 x 9 x 2-inch baking pan with nonstick vegetable-oil cooking spray.
2. Stir together flour, baking powder and salt in bowl.
3. Whirl almonds in food processor until finely ground. Add butter and vanilla. Whirl until well blended. Add flour mixture and sugar. Whirl to mix.

Reserve ½ cup mixture for topping. Add egg to remaining flour mixture in container of food processor. Whirl until well combined and dough forms. Press dough over bottom of prepared pan.
4. Bake in 375° oven for 10 minutes or until lightly browned; cool slightly.
5. Spread raspberry preserves over dough. Sprinkle with reserved crumb mixture in diagonal strips across top.
6. Bake 12 minutes more or until top is golden brown. Cool in pan on wire rack. Cut into bars to serve.
Yield: Makes 24 bars.

CHOCOLATE-PECAN TOFFEE BARS

1 cup (2 sticks) butter, at room
  temperature
1 cup sugar
1 egg yolk
1 teaspoon vanilla
2 cups all-purpose flour
½ teaspoon salt
1 package (6 ounces) semisweet
  chocolate pieces
1 cup pecans, chopped

1. Heat oven to 350°. Generously coat a 13 x 9 x 2-inch baking pan with nonstick vegetable-oil cooking spray.
2. Beat together butter, sugar, egg yolk and vanilla in medium-size bowl until well blended. Mix in flour and salt. Press mixture into an even layer in bottom of prepared baking pan.
3. Bake in 350° oven for 20 minutes or until top is golden brown. Remove to wire rack. Immediately sprinkle chocolate pieces over top. Let stand for 5 minutes to melt. Spread chocolate smoothly over top with metal spatula. Sprinkle with pecans. Cool completely. Cut into bars to serve.
Yield: Makes 24 bars.

*P*ass the petite treats (opposite, from top): Cran-Nut Mini Bundt Cakes, Cookies-And-Cream Cupcakes, Raspberry Crumb Bars (left), and Chocolate-Pecan Toffee Bars (right). Since they're so small, you can surely have more than one!

winter wonderland
(pages 6-13)

SNOWFLAKE TREE TOPPER AND PLACE MAT

You need: Tin snowflake forms; sandpaper; spray paints – matte white, blue metallic silver, mauve and multicolor glitter.

Making snowflakes: Sand tin forms. Apply one coat of matte white spray paint to both sides; let dry. Paint as desired on both sides with blue and mauve paints; let dry.

Finishing: Apply light coat of glitter paint to right side of form; let dry.

PIPE CLEANER SNOWFLAKES

You need (for each): One 12mm x 15mm 1" bump chenille stem; one 12mm x 10mm 3" bump chenille stem; metallic silver pom-pom; $^1/_4$ yd narrow sheer ribbon; glue gun.

Assembling: Cut each stem in half. Cross 1" bump stems at center; wrap a 3" bump stem around center. Bend spokes so they are evenly spaced. Glue pom-pom in center. Glue ribbon ends to center back for hanging loop.

STAR GARLAND

You need: Purchased pâpier-maché star garland; white spray paint; spray glitter; silver paint pen.

Decorating: Paint garland with several coats of white paint; let dry after each coat. Spray some stars with glitter; let dry. Use paint pen to add dots to remaining stars.

CHENILLE SNOWBALLS

You need: Old white chenille bedspread or crafts cuts of vintage-reproduction chenille; fiberfill stuffing; $^1/_2$"W ribbon.

Making each snowball: Cut a 5" circle from chenille. Sew running stitches $^1/_4$" from raw edge of circle; pull up slightly. Place a handful of stuffing in center. Pull up thread; add stuffing as needed. Tuck in raw edges; make several small stitches to secure gathers.

Finishing: Cut 6" of ribbon for each snowball; stitch ends over gathers to make hanging loop.

REGAL BLUE STOCKING

You need: Crinkle-satin fabrics – $^1/_2$ yd dark blue, $^1/_4$ yd light blue; $^1/_2$ yd white cotton fabric; $^3/_4$ yd silver snowflake trim; glue gun.

Cutting: Enlarge pattern (page 117). From dark blue fabric, cut stocking front and back. From cotton, cut lining front and back. From light blue fabric, cut one 7" x 28" cuff.

Sewing: *All stitching is done in $^1/_2$" seams, with right sides facing and raw edges even, unless noted.* Stitch stocking front to stocking back, leaving upper edge open. Stitch lining front to lining back, leaving upper edge open and leaving a 4" opening along back edge. Clip curves; trim seams. Stitch stocking to lining at upper edge, keeping seams aligned. Trim seams. Turn lining and stocking through opening; push lining into stocking. Stitch short ends of cuff together, forming a loop. Press under $^1/_4$", then $^1/_4$" again, on each long edge of cuff. Stitch close to pressed edges to hem cuff. Machine sew basting stitches along center of cuff; pull up threads to gather cuff to fit stocking. Baste gathered stitches of cuff to stocking, about $^1/_4$" below upper edge. Stitch in place along basting.

Finishing: On outside, glue trim over gathering stitches. Cut a 7" piece of remaining trim; fold in half to form hanging loop. Stitch ends of loop inside upper back corner of stocking to make hanging loop.

APPLIQUÉD THROW

You need: $1^1/_2$ yds of 54"W blue angora fabric; fusible white fabric snowflakes in assorted sizes; soft cloth.

Assembling: Turn under $^1/_4$", then $^1/_2$" on raw edges of fabric; press. Stitch close to folds to hem throw. Cut out and arrange snowflakes on right side of throw. Following manufacturer's directions, fuse snowflakes onto throw. Using cloth, fluff throw around snowflakes to remove iron imprint.

SILVER LEAF MIRROR

You need: Wood frame; acrylic and stencil paints in desired contrasting colors; paintbrushes – flat, stencil; masking tape; small stencils; foam core board; pencil; silver leaf; silver adhesive size; soft cloths; crafts knife; cutting mat; metal-edge ruler; brads; hammer.

Painting frame: Paint frame with several coats of acrylic paint, letting dry after each coat. Tape stencil on frame; using stencil brush, pounce stencil paint onto frame, working from edges of stencil to center. Let dry.

Making mirror: Place frame on foam core board; trace around outline. Following manufacturer's directions, apply size to board, extending slightly past outlines. Tear silver leaf into small pieces. When size has dried until clear and tacky, apply leaf to board. Let dry; rub with soft cloth to burnish. Re-mark frame dimensions in center of board; cut with crafts knife to make mirror.

Finishing: Place mirror in frame; secure edges with brads.

Misty-Gray, Ice-Blue and Regal Blue Stockings

1 square = 1"

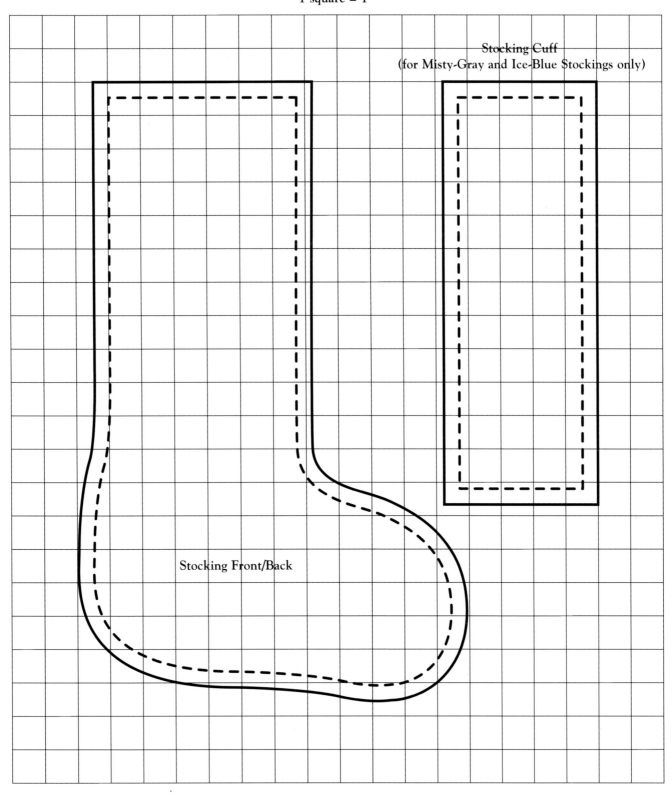

Stocking Cuff
(for Misty-Gray and Ice-Blue Stockings only)

Stocking Front/Back

Mini Skates

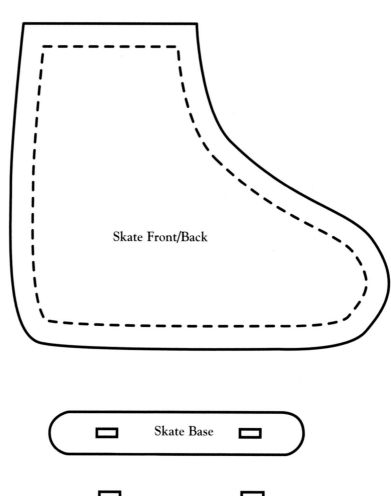

Skate Front/Back

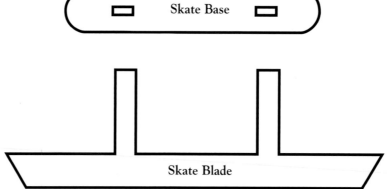

Skate Base

Skate Blade

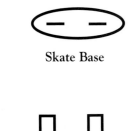

Skate Base

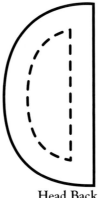

Head Back

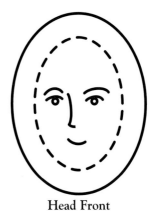

Head Front

Skate Blade

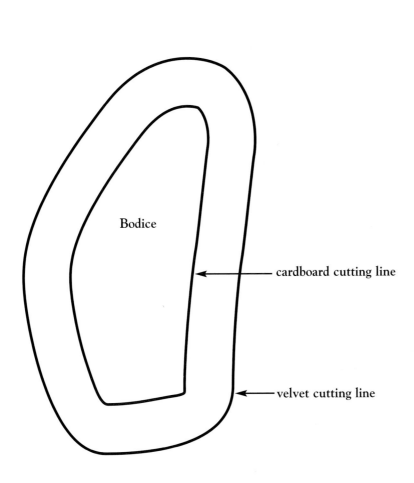

Bodice

← cardboard cutting line

← velvet cutting line

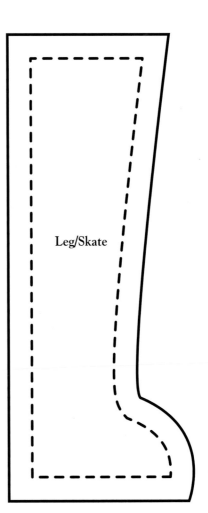

Leg/Skate

HOLIDAY SPOTLIGHT:
winning window boxes
(pages 14-15)

BIRDHOUSE WINDOW BOX

You need: 1" x 8" common pine, 20' total; handsaw; saber saw; wood glue; hammer; 1$\frac{1}{2}$" finishing nails; drill with bit; wood screws; two purchased decorative birdhouses; paintbrushes; acrylic paint – red, green, white, yellow; clear polyurethane.

Cutting wood: *Front* – Cut one piece 65$\frac{1}{2}$"L. *Back* – Cut one piece 65$\frac{1}{2}$"L. *Bottom* – Cut one piece 64"L. *Sides* – Cut two pieces each 6$\frac{1}{2}$"W x 7$\frac{1}{4}$"L. Creating your own scallop (see photo, page 14) cut out decorative front panel piece.

Assembling box: Glue/nail front to outer edge of bottom piece ($\frac{3}{4}$" is exposed at each end of bottom piece). Glue/nail back to bottom, same as front. Glue/nail sides. Glue decorative scallop to front.

Attaching birdhouses: Drill pilot holes in sides, then screw on birdhouses.

Painting: Paint box green; wipe off excess while wet; let dry. Paint scallop and birdhouses red; add freehand wreaths and other details. When dry, apply two coats of polyurethane.

CHICKEN-WIRE WINDOW BOX

You need: $\frac{1}{2}$" dia wood dowels – two pieces 36"L; saw; 36"L wood shelf; drill with $\frac{1}{2}$" bit; paintbrush; wood glue; wood stain; polyurethane; wire cutters; chicken wire; staple gun; 20-gauge wire.

Cutting dowels: Cut ten 7"L pieces.

Inserting dowels in shelf: Along both long sides of shelf, measure and divide length into five equal sections; mark. At marks, drill $\frac{1}{4}$" deep holes for dowels. Brush glue on one end of each dowel; insert in holes. Let set.

Staining: Brush stain on shelf and dowels; dry. Brush on polyurethane.

Adding chicken wire: Cut individual pieces for front, back and sides, each slightly longer than the width or depth of planter; height, from top of dowels to bottom edge of shelf. Staple bottom edge of chicken wire along edge of shelf, wrapping ends around dowels at corners. Cut 3"L pieces of 20-gauge wire; use to secure chicken wire to dowels.

PICKET FENCE PLANTER

You need: Wooden planter box; 12"H wooden picket-style garden edging; wire cutters; handsaw; wood glue; small branches; 1" finishing nails; hammer; white spray paint; burnt umber acrylic paint; flat paintbrush.

Preparing pickets: Use wire cutters to cut wire from garden edging. Use saw to cut individual pickets to desired heights.

Assembling: Glue/nail pickets to planter box. Attach branches in same manner.

Finishing: Spray planter with white paint; let dry. Lightly dry-brush burnt umber paint over box to give an aged look.

happy hues (pages 16-21)

EXTRA-BRILLIANT BALLS

You need: Plain porcelain ball ornaments; desired colors acrylic paints; paintbrushes; craft glue; glitter.

Painting: Paint balls with desired color basecoat. When dry, add freehand details.

Finishing: Apply glue to balls in desired designs. Shake glitter over glue. When dry, shake off excess glitter.

STAR ORNAMENTS

You need: Purchased wooden star cutouts; gold and desired colors of acrylic paint; paintbrushes; assorted beads and sequins; jewel glue.

Painting: Paint stars with desired color basecoat. When dry, add gold details by dry brushing gold across entire ornament, adding dots, or painting points of stars.

Finishing: Glue beads and sequins to stars as desired.

POCKET STOCKING (continued)

Stitching pocket: *When sewing, place pieces right sides together and use 1/2" seam.* Leaving an opening for turning, sew pocket pieces together. Turn. Pin pocket on right side of one stocking piece. Arrange ribbons, button and trims on pocket as desired, folding under raw edges. Stitch trims and pocket to stocking, leaving top edge of pocket open.

Stitching stocking: Center rickrack over side/bottom stitching line on right side of one stocking piece; baste. Sew stocking pieces together, leaving top edge open. Turn. Center rickrack around stocking over top edge stitching line on right side; baste.

Adding lining and hanger: *Lining* – Sew lining pieces together, leaving top edge open. Do not turn. Insert lining in stocking (wrong sides facing) with cut edges even, seams matching. *Hanger* – Fold a 7" length of ribbon in half. With all raw edges even, place hanger in stocking; pin hanger ends to upper back edge of lining.

Adding cuff: Press under 1/2" on one long (bottom) edge of cuff. Arrange ribbons and trims on cuff as desired; stitch in place. Stitch short ends of cuff together, making a loop. Position cuff inside stocking with right side of cuff facing right side of lining and raw edges even. Stitch cuff to stocking. Fold cuff down over stocking.

LATTICE STOCKING

You need: 1/2 yd green silk for stocking; 1/2 yd desired fabric for lining; 24" of 2"W wired red velvet ribbon for cuff; 2 yds of 7/8"W green velvet ribbon for lattice and hanger; 1/2 yd each beaded tassel trim and metallic/ribbon trim; 1 5/8 yds red/metallic piping.

Cutting fabric: Enlarge pattern (page 125); add 1/2" seam allowance before cutting out. Fold stocking fabric in half. Use pattern to cut two stockings from folded fabric. Repeat to cut two stocking linings.

Creating lattice: Pin lengths of velvet ribbon on right side of front stocking piece, diagonally in crisscross fashion, spacing about 4" apart. Topstitch.

Stitching stocking: With raw edges matching, baste piping along side/bottom edge on right side of one stocking piece. Sew stocking pieces together, leaving top edge open. Turn. With raw edges matching, baste piping around top edge of stocking.

Adding lining and hanger: *Lining* – Sew lining pieces together, leaving top edge open. Do not turn. Insert lining in stocking (wrong sides facing) with cut edges even, seams matching. *Hanger* – Fold a 7" length of ribbon in half. With all raw edges even, place hanger in stocking; pin hanger ends to upper back edge of lining.

Adding cuff: Gather one long edge of wired ribbon to 14"L. Arrange beaded and metallic trim over gathered ribbon edge; topstitch. Stitch short ends of cuff together, making a loop. Position cuff inside stocking with right side of cuff facing right side of lining, matching raw edges to ungathered ribbon edge. Gather ribbon edge to fit stocking opening. Stitch cuff to stocking. Fold cuff down over stocking.

KNITTED BRIGHT STOCKING

You need: Wool yarn, 50 gram hanks, 2 hanks orange and 1 hank magenta; double pointed needles (dpn), one set (4 needles), size 7 OR SIZE NEEDED TO OBTAIN GAUGE; stitch marker; tapestry needle; crochet hook, size G/6; ball ornaments.

Gauge: In st st (K on RS; p on WS), 22 sts and 31 rows = 5". TAKE THE TIME TO CHECK YOUR GAUGE.

Cuff: Beg at top edge on one needle and magenta, cast on 52 sts. Divide sts on three needles. Join; take care not to twist sts on needles. Mark end of every rnd with a stitch marker. Work in rnds of seed st as follows: *Rnd 1* – *K1, p1, rep from * to end. *Rnd 2* – *P1, k1; rep from * to end. Rep last two rnds until cuff measures 5 1/2"L.

Stocking: Working in st st, dec 4 sts evenly across next rnd – 48 sts, dividing rem sts evenly on needles. Change to orange and continue in st st, work until leg measures 13 3/4"L from beg of st st rnds.

Heel: Sl 16 sts from first needle onto empty needle, then sl last 8 sts from third needle onto other end of the same needle – 24 heel sts. Divide rem 24 sts onto two needles to be worked later for instep. Cutting yarn and reattaching at beg of row, work back and forth in rows on heel sts only as follows: *Row 1 (WS)* – Sl 1 purlwise, purl to end. *Row 2 (RS)* – Sl 1 purlwise; knit to end. Rep these two rows until heel measures 2", end with a RS row.

Turn heel: *Next Row (WS)* – Sl 1, p14, p2tog, p1, turn. *Row 2* – Sl 1, k7, SKP, k1, turn. *Row 3* – Sl 1, p8, p2tog, p1, turn. *Row 4* – Sl 1, k4, SKP, k1, turn. Continue in this way, always having one more st before dec on every row until 16 sts rem.

Shape instep: *Next rnd (RS)* – With same needle pick up and k 8 sts along side of heel piece (Needle 1); with Needle 2, k next 24 sts (instep); with Needle 3, pick up and k 8 sts along other side of heel piece, then with same needle, k 8 sts from Needle 1. There are16 sts on Needles 1 and 3; 24 sts on Needle 2 for a total of 56 sts. Mark center of heel for end of rnd. Continue as follows: *Rnd 1* – *Needle 1* k to last 3 sts, k2tog, k1; *Needle 2:* knit; *Needle 3:* k1, SKP, k to end. *Rnd 2* – Knit. Rep last two rnds 3 times more – 48 sts. Continue to work even until foot measures 8" from back of heel to beg of shape toe.

Shape toe: *Rnd 1* – *Needle 1:* k to last 3 sts, k2tog, k1; *Needle 2:* k1, SKP, k to last 3 sts, k2tog, k1; *Needle 3:* k1, SKP, k to end. *Rnd 2* – Knit. Rep last two rnds 7 times more – 16 sts. Place 8 sts on two needles and weave tog using Kitchener st.

Finishing: *Making hanging loop* – With orange, cast on 4 sts, do not turn. *Sl sts to other end of needle and k4; rep from * until cord measures 5¹/₂"L. Bind off. Join ends; sew inside stocking. Fold over cuff; sew on balls.

Knit Abbreviations
beg = begin, beginning
dec(s) = decrease(s)
" = inch(es)
inc = increase
k = knit
p = purl
rem = remaining
rep = repeat
RS = right side
rnd(s) = round(s)
SKP = sl 1, knit 1, pass slip stitch
    over knit stitches
sl = slip
st(s) = stitch(es)
st st = stockinette stitch
tog = together
work even = work without inc or dec
WS = wrong side
* = repeat whatever follows the * as
    many times as specified
( ) = contains explanatory remarks

Monogrammed Stocking
1 square = 1"

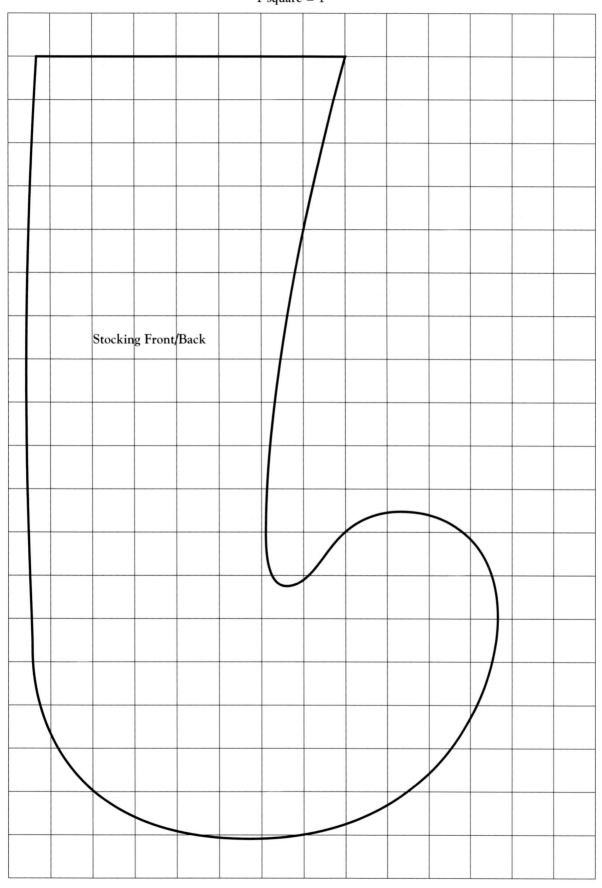

Stocking Front/Back

Pocket Stocking
1 square = 1"

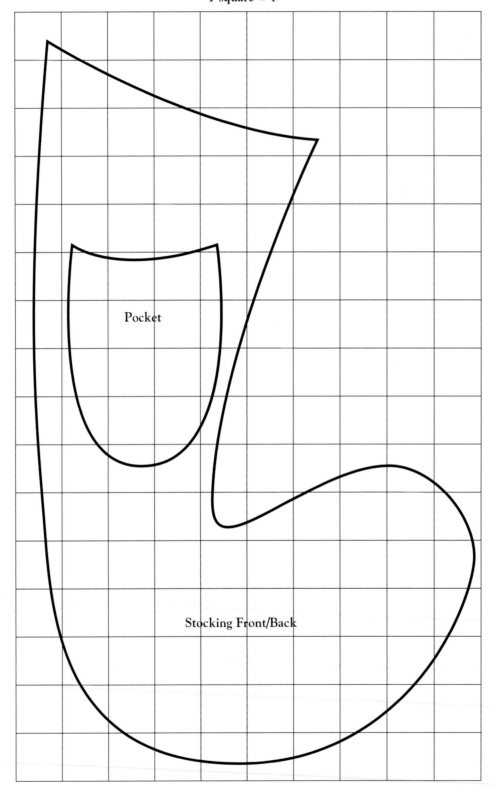

Pocket

Stocking Front/Back

Lattice Stocking
1 square = 1"

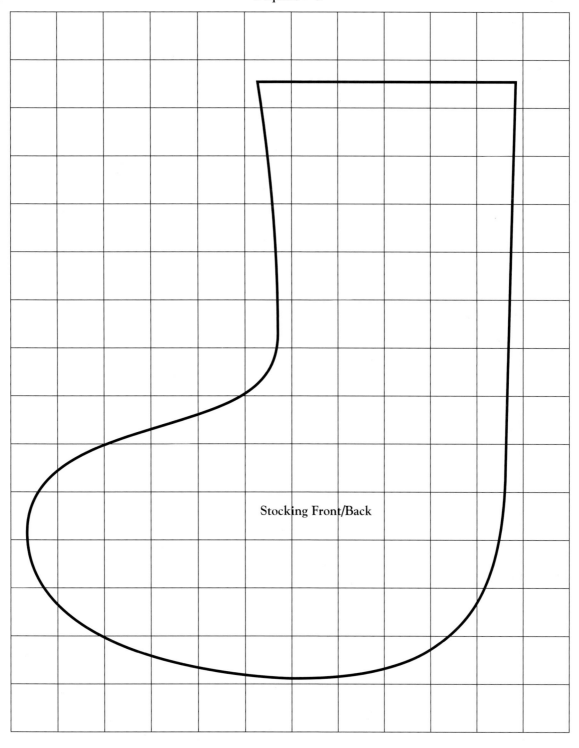

Stocking Front/Back

HOLIDAY SPOTLIGHT:
a round of wreaths
(pages 22-23)

CHEF'S WREATH

You need: 18" grapevine wreath; woven raffia ribbon; glue gun; artificial berry clusters; florist's wire; copper molds; glass vegetable ornaments; mini ladle; cinnamon sticks; bread wrapper ties; dried red chilies; sprigs of fresh herbs.

Assembling: Wrap a length of ribbon around wreath; glue ends to back of wreath. Insert or wire berry clusters into wreath. Use florist's wire or wrapper ties to attach molds, ornaments and ladle to wreath. Tie a bundle of cinnamon sticks together with wrapper tie; wire to wreath. Use florist's wire to wire a group of chilies together to form a star shape; wire to wreath. Tie remaining ribbon in multi-loop bow. Wire to wreath. Insert herbs into wreath.

Finishing: Cut 15" of wire; fold in half, then twist together along length to make hanging loop. Twist ends of loop through upper back of wreath.

APPLE WREATH

You need: 11 yds of 16-gauge rebar tie wire; dried apple slices; artificial apples – red, green; artificial leaves; 2 yds of $2^1/4$"W wire-edge ribbon; 22-gauge florist's wire (for bow); glue gun (optional).

Making wreath: Wind tie wire loosely into an 18" circle, adding loops and bending wire into a freeform wreath shape; twist ends together.

Decorating wreath: Insert dried apples, artificial apples and leaves between bends of wire wreath, using glue to secure if needed. Tie ribbon in a multi-loop bow; secure with florist's wire. Wire bow to wreath.

SILVER LEAVES WREATH

You need: Wire wreath form; silver spray paint; tracing paper; several packages of aluminum craft foil; stylus (or ball-point pen without ink); awl or small nail; small buttons (without shanks); 22-gauge silver spool wire.

Preparing wreath and buttons: Spray wreath and buttons with silver paint; let dry.

Making leaves: Trace full-size leaf pattern (below) onto tracing paper. Place craft foil on a thick layer of newspapers with pattern on top. Use stylus and firm pressure to trace leaf pattern, including veins, onto foil. Cut out along outer edges using scissors. Use awl to make two holes at base of leaf, about $1/8$" apart. Thread an 8" length of wire through a button, then through holes in leaf (button keeps wire from ripping through foil). Twist wire close to leaf. Make as many leaves as desired, in the same manner.

Finishing: Use wire "stems" to wire leaves to wreath form.

Silver Leaves Wreath – Leaf

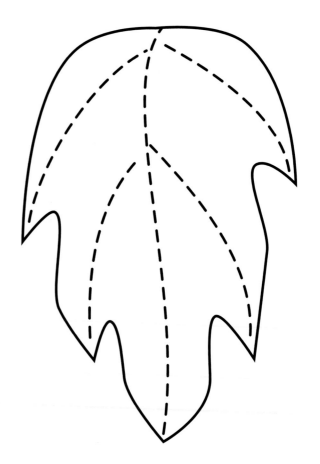

tidings of comfort and joy
(pages 24-31)

PAPER VOTIVE HOLDERS

You need: 12" high cylindrical glass votive candle holders; color photocopies of assorted Christmas images, musical images, child's Christmas-book illustrations, sheet music and alphabets; pinking shears; spray-mount adhesive; paper crimper.

Making collage holder: Cut out desired images; trim edges with pinking shears. Spray backs of paper with adhesive; smooth onto holder, overlapping edges. Cut out and glue on letters in same manner.

Making storybook votive holder: Cut out desired images from child's book; trim edges with pinking shears. Spray backs of paper with adhesive; smooth onto holder, overlapping edges. Cut out and glue on letters in same manner.

Making music candle "sleeve": Cut sheet music and music images into small pieces; trim edges with pinking shears. Spray backs of paper pieces with adhesive; smooth onto holder, overlapping edges. Cut additional paper about 2" wide and twice as long as holder circumference. Following manufacturer's directions, pass paper through crimper; glue around base of holder. Fold top edges of paper away from votive holder.

Note: Never leave burning candles unattended.

3-D PAPER ORNAMENTS

You need: Old hardcover book; medium-weight cardboard; crafts knife; cutting mat; lightweight cotton string; glue gun; assorted large beads.

Preparing book: Remove covers from book. Cut through spine to divide book into sections about 1/4" to 1/2" thick.

Cutting: Use full-size pattern (this page or page 128). Trace pattern onto cardboard; cut out. Open book section; place on cutting mat. Place pattern on section, aligning center dashed line of pattern with book spine. Using crafts knife, cut around pattern, cutting through a few pages at a time to keep cutting lines even.

Making ornament: Open pages in center; place binding side up on work surface. Cut four 12" pieces of string. Apply glue down spine; press strings into glue so they extend evenly at top and bottom of spine. Fluff pages on each side of strings. Apply more glue down spine; press sides together so ornament is round.

Finishing: String several beads onto each end of string. At bottom of ornament, tie strings around bottom bead to secure. At top of ornament, tie strings together at top of bead, then again several inches above bead to form hanging loop. Trim excess string at each end of ornament.

3-D Paper Ornaments

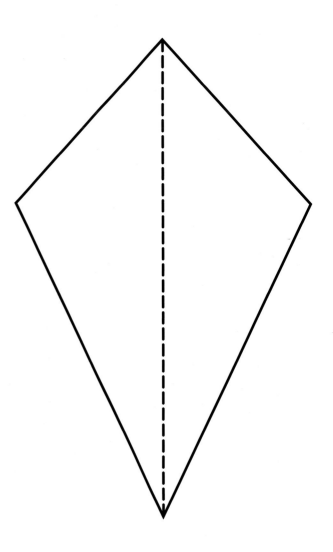

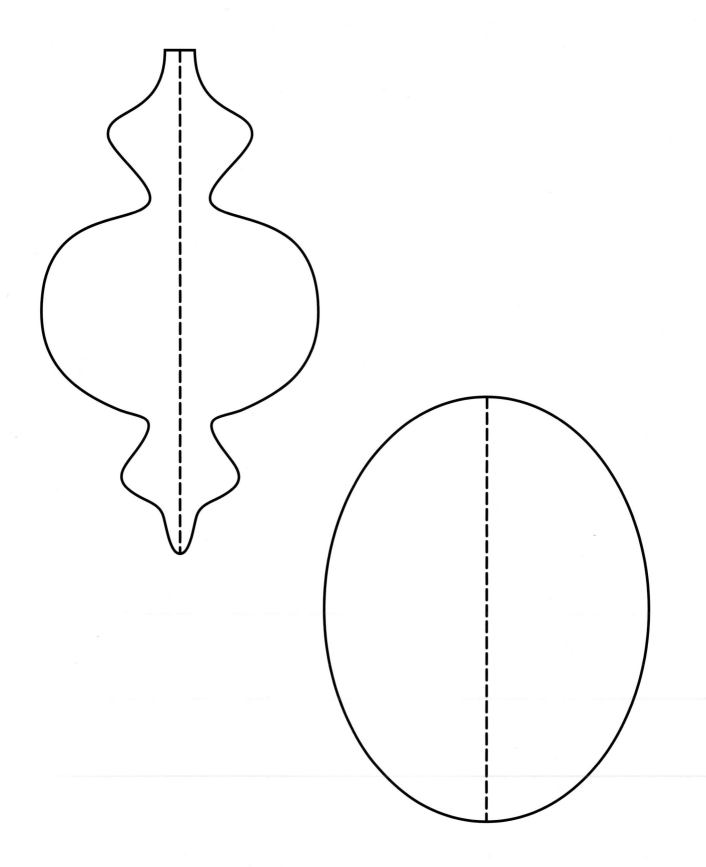

MOCK CHENILLE STOCKING

You need: One crafts-size piece of prequilted muslin.

Cutting: Enlarge pattern (page 130). Fold muslin in half, with quilted lines running horizontally; cut stocking front and back. Place pieces right side up. Slip scissor blade between batting and backing, between two stitching lines; cut through batting and upper layer of muslin. Cut between each set of stitching lines from lower edge of stocking to cuff area on each piece in same manner.

Sewing: Pin stocking front to back, with wrong sides facing and raw edges even. Stitch edges in 1/4" seams, leaving upper edge open. Fold cuff edge 1/2" to right side; stitch close to raw edge to hem cuff. Fold down cuff. Cut 1" x 7" piece of fabric for hanging loop. Fold in half crosswise; stitch ends inside upper edge of stocking.

Finishing: Machine wash and dry stocking several times to fray cut edges of fabric, creating chenille effect.

SCARF STOCKING

You need: 1/2 yd red wool; plaid fringed wool scarf.

Cutting: Enlarge pattern (page 131). From red fabric, cut stocking front and back. From each end of scarf, cut a 7" long section, not including fringe, for cuff. Also cut 1" x 10" strip of plaid for hanging loop.

Sewing: With right sides up and upper edges even, pin cuff to top of each stocking section. Trim sides of cuff even with sides of stocking; baste cuff in place. Pin stocking front to back, with right sides facing and raw edges even. Stitch sides and lower edges in 1/4" seam, leaving upper edge open. Trim seams; turn. Turn under 1" on upper edge of stocking; slip-stitch hem in place.

Finishing: Fold loop in half; pin and stitch ends to upper back corner of stocking to make hanging loop.

JOY PILLOWS

You need (for set of 3 pillows): Wool fabrics – 5/8 yd each solid red, tan tartan, tan window-pane check; heavy white cotton cord; chalk marking pencil; fabric glue; three 15" square pillow forms.

Cutting: For "J," cut one 22" square each of red and tartan wools for front and back. For "O," cut two 18" squares of checked wool for front and back. For "Y," cut one 16" square each of red and tartan wool and four 3" x 15" fringe strips from tartan wool.

Sewing: *All stitching is done in 1/2" seams, with right sides facing and raw edges even, unless noted.* For "J," stitch front to back, leaving 10" opening on one side. Trim corners; turn. Press. Mark line 3" from each edge of pillow. Stitch along line through all layers to form flange, leaving an opening just below outer opening. Insert pillow form; finish machine-stitching inner line. Slip-stitch outer opening closed. For "O," stitch front to back in same manner. Mark flange line 1" from each edge; finish stitching and stuffing pillow in same manner. For

"Y," pin a fringe strip to each edge of front; baste. Pin and stitch front to back in same manner. Insert form; slip-stitch opening closed.

Finishing: Draw letter on each pillow, referring to photograph (page 31) for example. Apply glue to cover chalk lines. Press cord into glue, pinning in spots to secure. Let dry; remove pins.

FIREPLACE SCREEN

You need: One 32" x 40" piece of 1/2" pine board or plywood; wood primer; hand saw; sandpaper; crafts glue; 3/4"W masking tape; small sea sponge; ecru acrylic paint; stencil paints – burgundy, ecru, gold, red, green; pouncer-style foam paintbrushes; 2 sets of alphabet letter stencils – script, block; stencil adhesive.

Preparing board: For screen, cut 26" x 30" piece of board. Mark curved edge on board as desired, referring to photograph (page 31) for suggested shape. Using hand saw, cut along outline. From wood remnants, cut two 4" x 12" stands, cutting curve along one edge of each stand to shape top edges. In center of each top edge, cut 3"-deep slot about 5/8"W to support screen. Sand all edges of all pieces. Coat screen and stands with primer; let dry. Spread glue on cut edges of screen and stands; apply tape over glue, trimming tape even with edges of boards to seal edges.

Painting: Using ecru paint and pouncer or sea sponge, apply paint to all surfaces of screen and stands, applying paint at random for textured effect.

Stenciling: Decide upon desired words and spacing of words (see photo, page 31, for suggested design). Draw light pencil guidelines on front of screen for words. Spray wrong side of stencil with adhesive; place on screen. Using pouncers and paints, stencil words; let dry.

Finishing: Place screen in stands so stands are about 4" from ends.

Note: Keep screen away from lit fire.

Mock Chenille Stocking
1 square = 1"

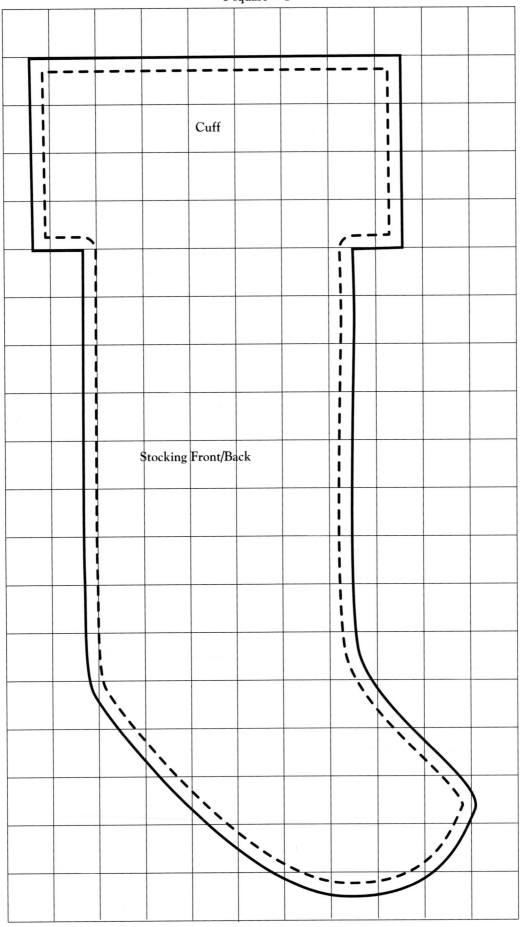

Cuff

Stocking Front/Back

Scarf Stocking
1 square = 1"

Stocking Front/Back

131

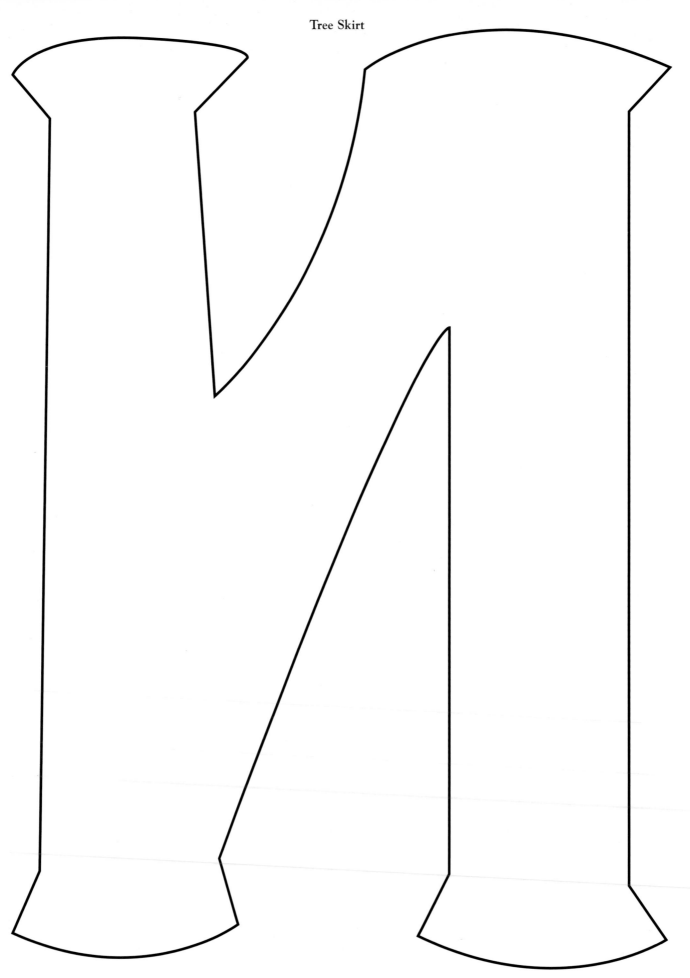

Tree Skirt

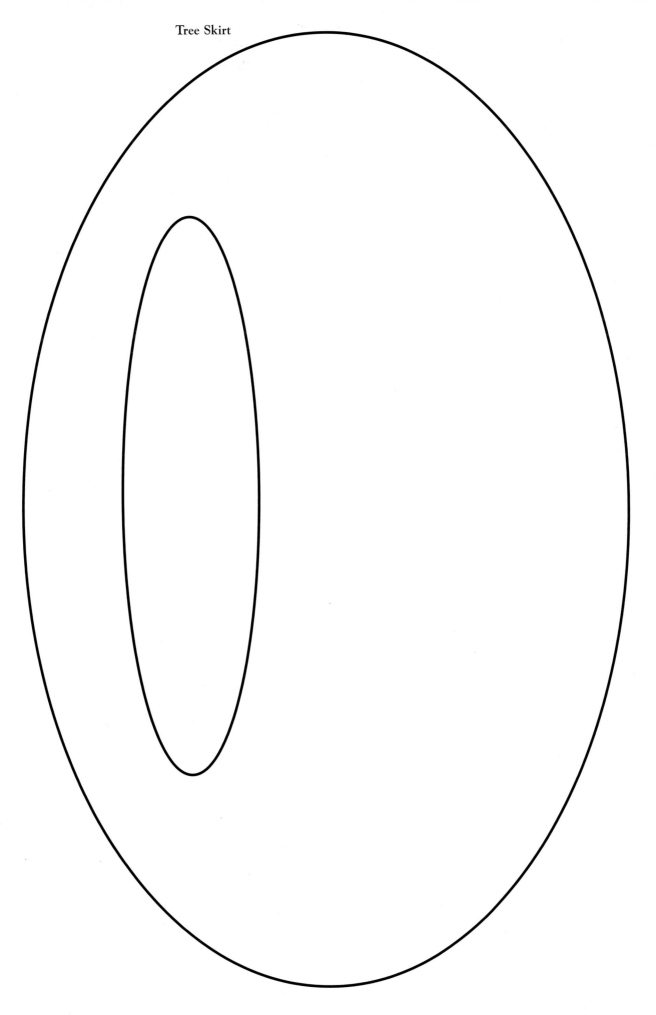

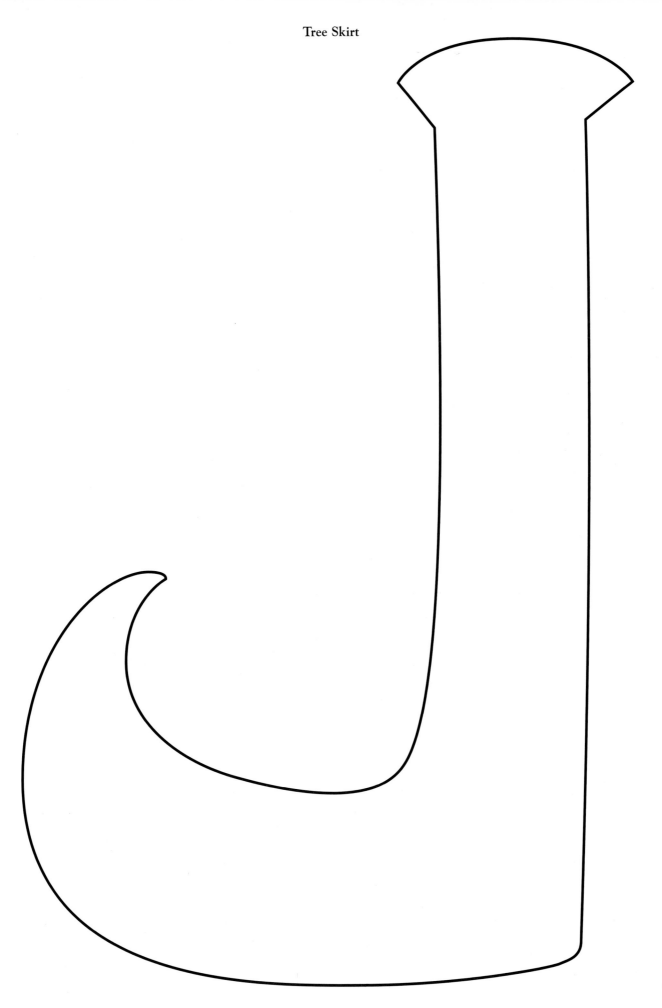

a touch of class:
rich red roses (pages 32-37)

WOVEN RIBBONS STOCKING (continued)

Assembling: With right sides facing, insert stocking into lining, aligning seams. Sew top edges together. Turn through opening in lining; slip-stitch opening closed. Push lining down into stocking.

RIBBON ROSE AND STAMPED VELVET STOCKING

You need: $^2/_3$ yd red velvet; rose rubber stamp; chalk pencil; $^2/_3$ yd red lining fabric; $^1/_4$ yd red moiré; 7 coiled ribbon roses with ribbon leaves.

Cutting pieces: Enlarge pattern (page 137.) From velvet, cut one 13" x 20" piece for stocking front, one stocking back, and one $2^1/_2$" x 7" strip for hanging loop. From lining fabric, cut two pieces for lining front and back. From moiré, cut one 10" x 14" cuff.

Embossing fabric: With chalk pencil, trace around stocking pattern on wrong side of 13" x 20" piece. Trace around edges of rubber stamp to establish a grid, making sure to extend grid beyond edges of stocking pattern. Place rubber stamp face up on ironing board and position right side of fabric against stamp, aligning grid markings with edges of stamp. Lightly mist wrong side of fabric with water, and press hot iron firmly against fabric for 20-40 seconds, until the pattern of the stamp becomes clear. Continue in same manner to stamp design in each grid square. Cut out stocking front.

Stitching stocking: *When sewing, place pieces right sides together and use $^1/_2$" seam, unless noted.* Sew stocking pieces together, leaving top edge open; turn. Sew lining pieces together, leaving top edge open; do not turn. Insert lining in stocking (wrong sides facing) with cut edges even, seams matching.

Making hanging loop: Fold loop strip in half lengthwise; stitch long edge in $^1/_4$" seam. Turn right side out; stitch close to both long edges. Fold loop in half crosswise; pin inside stocking lining at back edge, aligning raw edges of loop and lining.

Adding cuff: Stitch short ends of cuff together, making a loop. Fold cuff in half, wrong sides facing and matching raw edges. Position cuff inside stocking with raw edges even. Stitch cuff to stocking. Fold cuff down over stocking.

Finishing: Hand-stitch ribbon roses to front of cuff.

KISSING BALL

You need: Plastic foam ball; ribbon – $1^1/_2$ yds green, $^1/_2$ yd red; T-pin; artificial roses, flowers, mistletoe; low-temp glue gun.

To do: For hanging loop, fold 1 yd length of green ribbon in half; insert T-pin through ribbon ends. Apply glue to pin; insert pin into foam ball. Glue roses, flowers, and mistletoe to ball, covering completely. Tie remaining ribbons around base of hanging loop.

Ruffled and Rosy Stocking, Velvet Stocking with Ribbon Trimmed Cuff, Woven Ribbons Stocking and
Ribbon Rose and Stamped Velvet Stocking
1 square = 1"

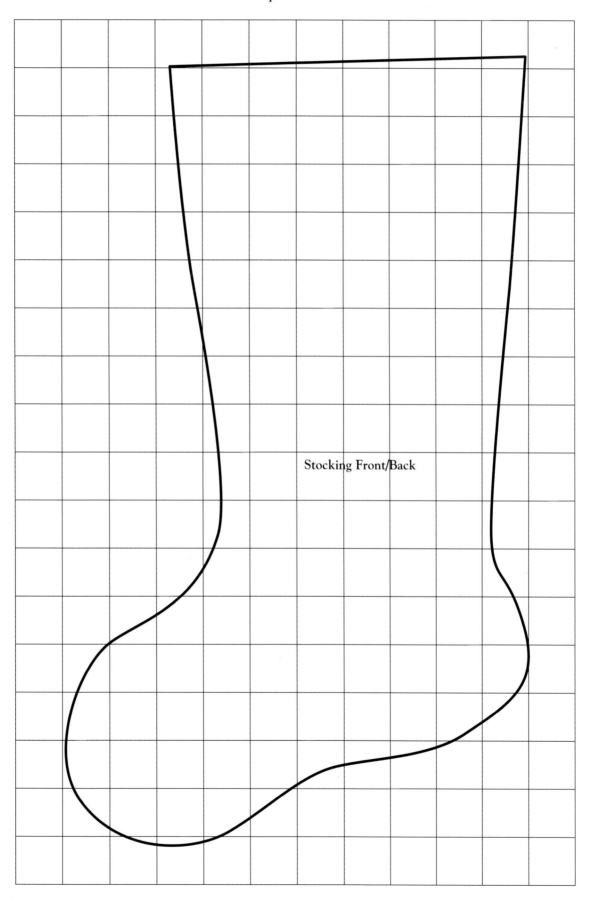

Stocking Front/Back

ORGANZA TREE SKIRT

You need: 3 yds orange organza; 1½ yds fuchsia taffeta; chalk marking pencil; 4 yds fuchsia ball fringe or sequin fringe trim.

Gathering organza: On one long edge, gather up small sections of organza between fingers; make several small stitches by hand to secure gathers. Continue gathering and stitching organza in same manner until organza is about 1½ yds long. Set dry iron to silk setting; press to secure pleats.

Making skirt: Fold taffeta in quarters. Mark curved line 22" from folded corner; cut along line to form circle. Mark curved line 3" from folded corner; cut along line to form center opening. Open out taffeta; place on organza, right sides facing. Pin layers together. Stitch ¼" from outer edge of taffeta. Stitch ¼" from edge of center opening. Trim organza even with taffeta along both stitching lines. Cut through both layers from outer edge to center opening to form back opening of skirt. Stitch ¼" from each edge, leaving a 10" opening along one straight edge. Clip curves; turn right side out. Slip-stitch opening closed.

Finishing: Pin ball fringe along outer edge of skirt; slip-stitch from wrong side of skirt.

BEADED FINIALS

You need (for each): Wooden finial with top loop; water-based gold-leaf size; paintbrushes; gold leaf; soft cloths; paper-backed double-sided tape; assorted bugle, seed and micro beads; ¼ yd ribbon.

Decorating: Following manufacturer's directions, apply size to finial where gold leaf is desired. Tear leaf into small uneven pieces. Allow size to dry until clear and tacky, then apply leaf to finial. Allow to dry; rub with soft cloth to burnish. Apply tape to remaining areas of finial. Where tape layers overlap, remove backing before attaching next layer. Remove all backing; press larger beads onto tape, making sure beads are as flush to surface as possible. Press smaller beads into remaining spaces.

Finishing: Slip ribbon through loop at top; tie ends in bow.

GIFT PACKAGE PLACE MATS (continued)

Making sides: Stitch side strips to each side of a 1½" ribbon strip in same manner. Cut one end of this strip at a 45-degree angle. Measure and mark strip at 9¾" intervals starting at this angled edge; cut four parallelograms along these marks for package sides.

Making tops: Stitch top strips to each side of each remaining 1½" ribbon strip in same manner. Cut one end of this strip at a 45-degree angle, cutting in opposite direction from side strips. Stitch 1¼" ribbon strip to one angled end of one strip, allowing excess ribbon to extend at ends. Press seam allowance toward ribbon; trim ribbon even with ends of parallelogram. Stitch second parallelogram for package top to other side of ribbon strip in same manner. Make three more package tops in same manner.

Assembling top: Pin a top to each side along angled edge; stitch from point to inside corner, stopping ¼" from corner. Press seam allowances toward top. Pin this top/side section to front, matching ribbon strips. Stitch, pivoting stitching at corner to make place mat top.

Assembling mat: Place batting on work surface; place back, right side up, and top, right side down, on batting. Stitch edges, leaving opening along one edge. Trim seams; turn right side out. Slip-stitch opening closed.

Quilting: Thread machine with nylon thread on top and thread to match backing in bottom. Stitch along seam lines through all layers.

Making bows: Fold loop strip in half lengthwise; stitch long edge. Turn right side out; press, centering seam. Cut four 3" pieces from tube for loops (discard excess). Overlap ends of each loop to form small tubes; slip-stitch ends together. Hand-stitch loops to center top of each package. Pin and stitch two bow squares together, leaving opening along one edge. Trim corners; turn right side out. Press; slip-stitch opening closed. Hand-pleat center of each bow; slip each through a loop.

LIGHTBULB PLACE CARDS

You need: Small tin lightbulb forms; sandpaper; masking tape; spray paints – yellow, green; fine-point permanent marker; narrow ribbon.

Decorating: Sand forms. Apply tape around socket portion of form. Spray top of form with two or more coats of yellow paint on front and back; let dry. Remove tape. Apply tape over painted portion of form. Spray socket portion of form with two or more coats of green paint on front and back; let dry. Remove tape.

Finishing: Using marker, write initials on form. Cut 10" of ribbon; tie in bow around base of form.

Holiday Stockings
1 square = 1"

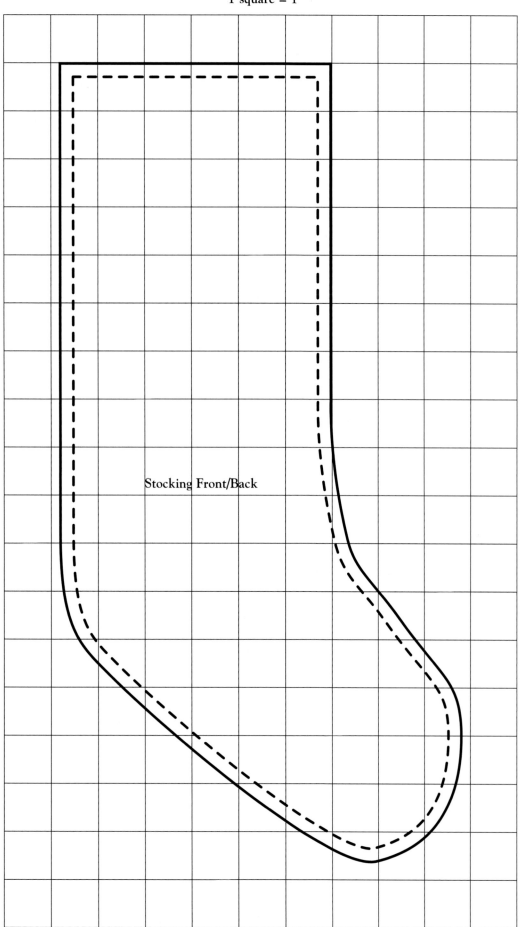

Stocking Front/Back

HOLIDAY SPOTLIGHT:
candles all aglow
(pages 46-47)

PIERCED-TIN TREES

You need: Pillar candle in desired size; heavy-duty scissors; sheets of aluminum flashing; awl; one self-adhesive hook-and-loop fastener circle.

Making pattern: Draw desired height tree on a piece of paper. To bottom of tree, add a band 1"W and 1" longer than circumference of candle. Cut out pattern.

Assembling: Place pattern on flashing; draw around outline with pencil. Cut out along outline. Using awl, poke designs in tree as desired. Place one half of fastener circle on each end of band; wrap around base of candle and fasten ends. Adjust fastener placement if needed.

DECOUPAGED MOSAICS

You need: Tissue paper and foil in assorted bright colors; glass votive holder; paintbrush; decoupage medium; foam paintbrush.

Assembling: Cut papers into 1" squares; arrange on holder to test size and color arrangement. Trim if needed to create "tiles." Apply thin coat of medium to outside of votive; press tiles into position, leaving desired amount of space between pieces. Let dry. Apply several coats of medium over paper, letting dry after each coat.

GOLD LEAF CANDLES

You need: Felt-tip marker; tracing paper; masking tape; sheets of gold leaf; pillar candle; ballpoint pen or skewer.

Making patterns: Using marker, draw desired motifs on tracing paper.

Transferring motifs: Tape gold leaf, gold side down, to candle. Tape motif over gold leaf. Using pen, draw over motif to transfer gold leaf to candle. Peel back gold leaf to insure entire motif has been transferred. Remove motif and gold leaf. Using fresh sheets of gold leaf, repeat taping and transferring motifs to cover candle in same way. Do not place tape over areas where leaf has been applied.

STENCILED PILLARS

You need: Candle; stencil plastic and crafts knife (for motif stencils); flat lace trim (for lacy stencils); spray stencil adhesive; nontoxic spray paint.

Preparing motif stencil: Measure height and circumference of candle; mark dimensions on stencil plastic. Draw design on plastic to fit inside outlines. Cut out parts of design to make stencil.

Preparing lace: Measure circumference of candle. Cut lengths of lace this measurement.

Stenciling candle: Spray back of stencil or lace lengths with adhesive; press onto candle. Spray candle with paint; let dry. Remove stencil or lace.

TAPERS

You need: Beeswax tapers; kitchen parchment paper; crafts knife.

To do: Place tapers on a baking sheet lined with parchment paper. Place in 300° oven for about 10 minutes to slightly soften wax. Remove from oven and use knife to cut a $1/2$" deep slit in taper at an angle. Before removing knife from wax, tilt knife back to curl wax sliver. Repeat in same manner as desired.

country charm (pages 48-55)

FOLKSY FELT PILLOWS

You need (for both pillows): 1 yd paper-backed fusible web; felt – $1/2$ yd red, $1/2$ yd cream; 3 yds green jumbo rickrack; two 14" pillow forms.

Cutting pieces (for each): From red, cut two 15" squares. From cream, cut one 15" square.

Making pillow front: Enlarge pattern (page 134 or 135). Trace pattern onto paper side of fusible web; do not cut out. Follow manufacturer's instructions to fuse web to cream felt square. Cut out pieces. Arrange shapes on one red felt square; fuse in place. Topstitch along all edges of cream shapes using matching thread. Baste rickrack to right side of pillow front, $1/2$" from edges.

Assembling pillow: Place front and back right sides together. Sew pieces using a $1/2$" seam, leaving an opening for turning. Turn pillow. Insert pillow form into pillow. Slip-stitch opening closed.

Patchwork, Ladybug and Holly Stockings
1 square = 1"

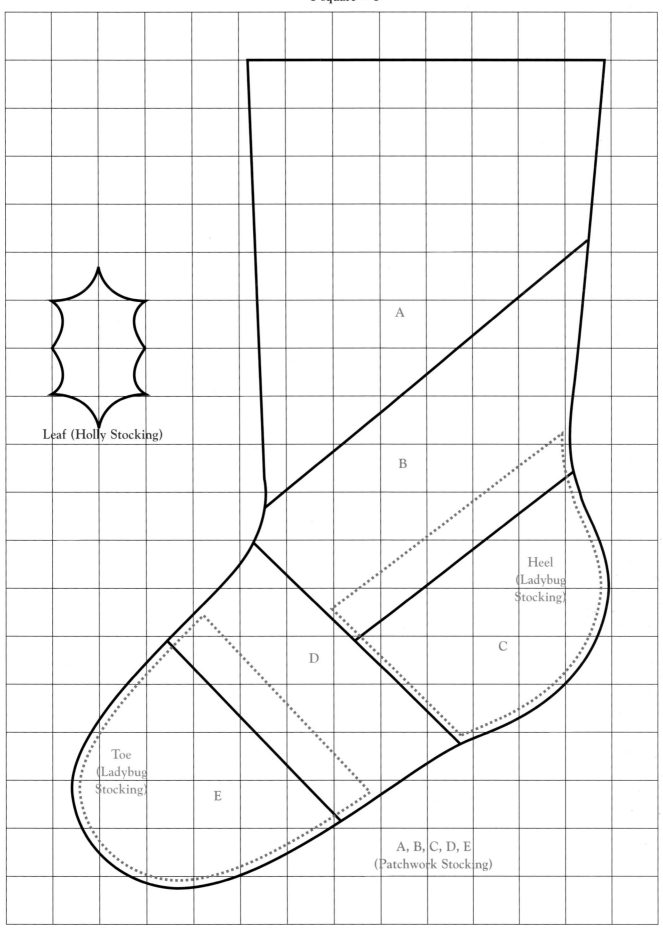

Leaf (Holly Stocking)

A

B

Heel
(Ladybug
Stocking)

C

D

Toe
(Ladybug
Stocking)

E

A, B, C, D, E
(Patchwork Stocking)

Chair-Back Heart and Heart Ornaments
1 square = 1"

Chair-Back Heart

Heart Ornament

HOLIDAY SPOTLIGHT:
it's a wrap
(pages 56-57)

FRINGE WRAP

You need: Gift wrap; crafts glue; ribbon.

To do: Cut four paper strips, each four times as long as gift height; overlap at 45-degree angles and glue at center (*Fig. 1*). Place gift in center; fold strips toward top (*Fig. 2*). Wrap ribbon just above gift (*Fig. 3*). Tie a bow with ribbon; fluff ends of strips (*Fig. 4*).

Fig. 1

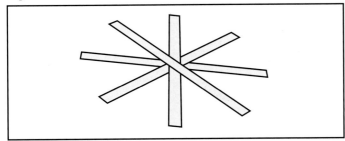

Fig. 2

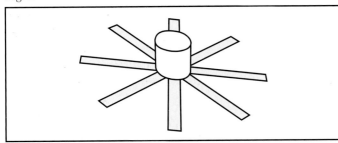

Fig. 3

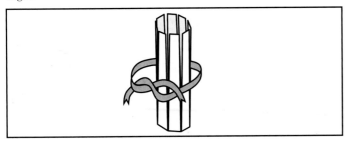

Fig. 4

TUXEDO WRAP

You need: Gift wrap; transparent tape; ribbon.

To do: Fold one end of the paper into pleats (*Fig. 1*). Secure pleated part by attaching tape to back (*Fig. 2*). Place paper so pleats appear on front of gift box; wrap box. Tie a ribbon lengthwise around box; make "bow tie" at top (*Fig. 3*).

Fig. 1

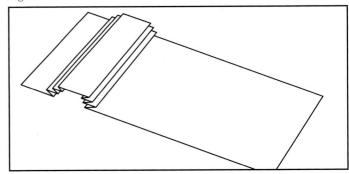

Fig. 2

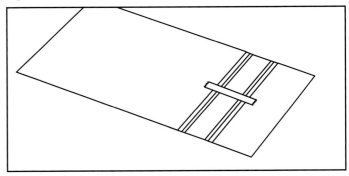

Fig. 3

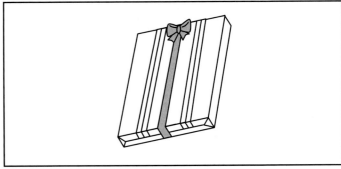

perfect presents (pages 59-65)

WOODEN BLOCKS AND BOX

You need: Nine 2" wood blocks; 7" square wood box; paintbrushes – foam, stencil; acrylic paints – antique white, red, mustard gold, metallic copper, metallic gold; crackle finish; gift wrap with holiday motifs; spray adhesive; lettering and small star stencils; masking tape; sandpaper; red marker; tan construction paper.

Decorating blocks: Paint blocks white; let dry. Paint one side of each block mustard; let dry. Following manufacturer's directions, coat mustard side with crackle finish and white paint; let dry. Tape "C" stencil over mustard side of one block. Pounce stencil brush in red or gold paint, then over stencil, to paint letter. Remove stencil; let dry. Stencil remaining blocks in same way, spelling out "Christmas." If desired, stencil letters to spell out recipient's name on other sides of blocks. Cut 2" squares of gift wrap, centering motifs. Spray back of square with adhesive; smooth onto a white side of block. Stencil metallic stars on all remaining sides of each block; let dry. Dip dry sponge brush in small amount of red paint and run along edges of each block; let dry. Sand lightly for aged effect.

Decorating box: Paint box and lid white; let dry. Paint edges red and sand same as for blocks. Write message on construction paper using marker. Tear paper to fit lid. Spray back of paper with adhesive; smooth onto top of box. Stencil metallic stars on all sides of box and lid; let dry.

Finishing: Place blocks in box, letters up, and replace lid.

PEN AND DESK SET

You need: Desk blotter; collage-style gift wrap or art paper; decoupage medium; foam brush; paper-backed double-sided tape; microbeads; ball point pen; tassel.

Decorating blotter: Cover work surface with newspaper to catch beads. Brush back of gift wrap with thin coat of decoupage medium; smooth over writing surface of blotter. Apply two coats of medium over top, letting dry after each coat. Cut desired images from gift wrap. Cover each side of desk blotter with tape; remove backing. Arrange images on tape; sprinkle microbeads over tape. Press beads into tape; shake off excess beads.

Decorating pen: Place tassel cord along pen so tassel extends at top. Cut end of tassel cord if it extends past tip of pen. Wrap tape around pen, over tassel cord; peel off backing. Roll pen in microbeads; press beads to adhere. Shake off excess.

VELVET MUFFLER

You need (for 17" x 47" muffler): 54"W velvet – four $\frac{1}{4}$ yd pieces of different colors or prints, one $\frac{2}{3}$ yd piece of another color or print.

Cutting: From large velvet piece, cut one 17$\frac{3}{4}$" x 47$\frac{3}{4}$" piece for backing; cut rest of this fabric, and other fabrics, into a total of forty-four 5" squares for patchwork.

Sewing patchwork: *All stitching is done in $\frac{3}{8}$" seams, with right sides facing and raw edges even, unless noted.* Pin patchwork squares together in four strips of 11 squares each, alternating colors and prints. Arrange pinned strips to form 4 x 11-square piece; check to ensure no adjacent squares are same color or print. Rearrange and pin squares as needed. Stitch squares in each strip together; press seams open. Pin and stitch strips together along long edges, aligning seams. Press seams open to make patchwork.

Making muffler: Pin and stitch patchwork to backing, leaving opening along one long side. Trim corners diagonally; turn. Slip-stitch opening closed.

SILK SHANTUNG PILLOWS

You need (for each): Silk shantung fabric – $\frac{3}{8}$ yd (large pillow), $\frac{1}{4}$ yd (small pillow); metallic and cotton threads to match fabric; fabric remnants; chalk pencil; fiberfill stuffing; 4 tassels.

Making yo-yos: Cut fabric remnants into 2$\frac{1}{2}$" circles (25 for large pillow, 4 for small). Sew hand running stitches around edge of each circle; pull up threads to gather, turning under raw edges as you pull. Make several small stitches at center, through all layers. Smooth into circle to make each yo-yo.

Cutting: From silk, cut two 13" squares (for large pillow) or two 9" squares (for small pillow) for pillow front and back.

Embroidering: For large pillow, draw 12$\frac{1}{2}$" square diagonally centered on wrong side of front. Divide square into 25 small squares by drawing four lines 2$\frac{1}{2}$" apart across square in each direction. For small pillow, draw 5" square diagonally centered on wrong side of front. Divide square into four small squares by drawing a line through center of square in each direction. Using matching metallic thread an wide machine zigzag stitch, sew over marked lines to make pillow front. Sew a yo-yo in center of each small square.

Sewing: Pin front to back, with right sides facing and raw edges even. Stitch edges in $\frac{1}{4}$" seams, leaving an opening along one edge; turn. Stuff; slip-stitch opening closed.

Finishing: Sew a tassel to each corner.

TRINKET-FILLED SOAPS

You need: Soap molds; clear glycerine bars; soap colors; glitter; soap scent; microwave-safe glass bowl; trinkets; rubbing alcohol in spray bottle.

Melting soap: Cut soap in cubes; put in bowl. Microwave 30 seconds, then at 5-second intervals if needed to melt.

Coloring: Stir in color, scent and glitter.

Adding trinkets: When film forms on soap, push film away and pour to coat bottom of mold. Let set 10 minutes; refrigerate an hour or until hard. Add trinket. Mist with alcohol. Fill with melted soap. Harden in refrigerator. Unmold.

Sweater Mittens
1 square = 1"

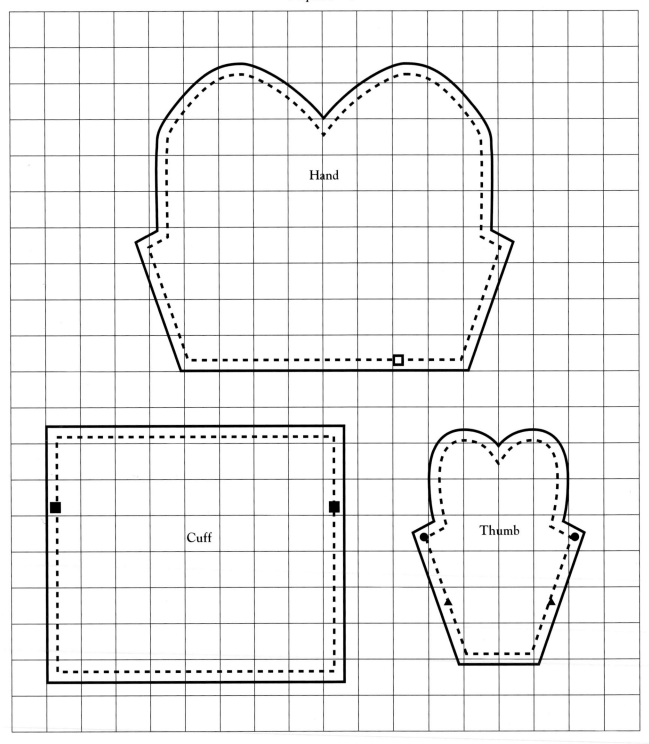

Hand

Cuff

Thumb

MISS HOLLY DOLL (continued)

Arms – Stitch each pair of arms together, leaving upper edge open. Clip curves; turn. Stuff firmly about three-quarters full; baste opening closed. Insert arms into body armholes; machine-stitch straight down to secure arms to body. *Legs* – Stitch and stuff legs same as arms; turn each leg to align seams before basting closed. Turn under $1/4$" on lower edge of body; press. Pin legs between body layers, near outer edges. Stuff body firmly; machine-stitch straight across, catching legs in stitching. Glue head to neck, aligning neck with mark on back of head; let dry. Slip-stitch head to body to secure.

Making hair: Cut 6" x 7" piece of cardboard; wrap yarn crosswise around cardboard until full. Slip-stitch yarn together across top of cardboard; slip off. Pin, then glue, hair across center back of head so hair hangs down back. Cut open loops; trim as desired. For topknot, wrap yarn lengthwise around 8" x 7" piece of cardboard, then stitch and slip yarn off cardboard in same manner. Glue hair across center back of head, covering top of first piece of hair. Pull hair up toward top of head, slightly off-center; wrap and tie additional yarn around topknot to secure. Cut loops open. For bangs, wrap hair crosswise around 2" x 5" piece of cardboard, then stitch and slip yarn off cardboard in same manner. Glue hair across forehead; cut open loops and trim as desired. Tie ribbon in bow around topknot. Apply blush to cheeks.

Making shirt: Stitch backs to front at shoulders and underarm seams. Stitch short ends of each cuff together. Stitch cuff to each sleeve, cuff seam aligned with underarm seam. Turn right side out; fold up cuffs. Turn under $1/2$" on neck edge; stitch close to fold to hem neck. Cut 1" piece of fastener tape; sew to upper back edges of shirt.

Making overalls: Sew zigzag stitches close to lower edge of each lining. Stitch lining to each overall section. Trim seams; turn linings to inside. Stitch overall sections together at side and inner leg seams. Clip curves; turn. Stitch pocket to lining, leaving small opening along one side. Trim corners; turn. Follow manufacturer's directions to fuse tree to center of pocket. Stitch a lining to each strap, leaving upper edge open. Clip curves; turn. Topstitch overalls, pocket and straps with yellow thread. Pin pocket to center front of overalls; stitch close to sides and lower edge. Pin curved ends of straps to overall bib; stitch button to each strap through all layers. Cut remaining fastener tape into two equal pieces; stitch pieces to back ends of straps and inside back of bib so straps will be adjustable. Dress doll in shirt and overalls.

Note: Doll contains small parts. Not suitable for children ages 3 and under.

MISS HOLLY'S STOCKING AND TOYS

You need: Felt – $1/4$ yd red, $1/4$ yd green, remnant of blue; $1/4$ yd red cotton lining fabric; desired fabric remnants for clown head, hat, body and ruffle; matching thread; $1/4$ yd fusible fabric stiffener; embroidery floss – cream, red, black; 2 small pom-poms; fiberfill stuffing; fabric glue; pinking shears; cosmetic blush.

Cutting: Enlarge patterns (pages 151-152). From red felt, cut two of each stocking stripe as marked. From green felt, cut two of each stocking stripe as marked and one cuff. From blue felt, cut two bear sections. From lining, cut stocking front and back lining. Cut two clown head sections, two clown body sections, 3" square for hat and one ruffle from desired fabrics. From stiffener, cut one cuff.

Making stocking: *All stitching is done in $1/4$" seams, with right sides facing and raw edges even, unless noted.* Stitch stripes together, alternating colors, for stocking front and back. Stitch front to back, leaving upper edge open. Stitch lining sections together in same manner, leaving additional opening 4" long along back edge. Stitch stocking to lining along upper edge. Turn right side out; slip-stitch opening closed. Push lining into stocking. Fuse stiffener onto wrong side of cuff. Glue cuff around upper edge of stocking, centering ends in back.

Making teddy bear: Cut 2" slit in center of back piece. Stitch front to back. Clip curves; turn. Stuff firmly; slip-stitch opening closed. Embroider cream mouth and eyes. Glue pom-pom nose in center of face.

Making clown: Cut 2" slit in center of back piece. Stitch front to back. Clip curves; turn. Stuff firmly; slip-stitch opening closed. Cut $1/2$" slit in center of head back; make head same as body. Glue, then stitch head to top of body. Embroider black eyes and red mouth. Glue pom-pom nose in center of face. Trim one long edge of collar with pinking shears. Sew hand gathering stitches along other long edge; pull up threads to gather collar to fit neck. Wrap and glue hat square around head. Wrap and tie floss around tip of hat. Apply blush to cheeks.

Note: Toys contain small parts. Not suitable for children ages 3 and under.

MRS. CLAUS BOXES

You need: 4 oval papier-mâché boxes in graduated sizes; wood pieces – 2 pine trees, two 1¹/₂" discs, one ¹/₂" round button; paintbrushes – sponge, flat, liner; acrylic paints – flesh, light red, white, green; crafts glue; satin-finish spray varnish; white curly doll hair; round doll glasses; fabrics – 1 yd small star print, ¹/₂ yd Santa print; 24" red ball fringe trim; 2 yds ¹/₂"W green satin ribbon; 2" x 3" piece of cardboard; small wiggle eyes; tissue paper; awl.

Assembling: *Boxes are numbered from smallest to largest.* Paint boxes as follows – box 1 rim with green, box 2 rim with white and bottom with flesh, box 3 rim and bottom with light red; let dry. Apply 2 coats of varnish to all painted surfaces. Place box 1 upside down. Crumple tissue paper; glue to bottom of box. From star fabric, cut oval 2" larger all around than box. Center fabric over paper, wrapping edges to inside of box; glue. Glue lid on box. Form star fabric, cut oval 1¹/₂" larger than lid 2. Glue fringe along edge of fabric to make cap. Paint discs and button with flesh for cheeks and nose. Apply small amount of light red to cheeks and nose; paint highlights on cheeks in white. Glue eyes, cheeks, and nose to box 2. Cut small pieces of hair; glue to top of lid 2. Place cap on top; trim hair as desired. Poke holes in sides of box 2; insert eye pieces of glasses through holes. Cut two 3" x 8" pieces of Santa-print fabric. Turn under long raw edges; glue. Glue strips over sides of box 3. Paint trees green; let dry. Cut ribbon in half. Tie one piece in bow. Glue trees and bow to box 3. Cut star fabric 2" wider and 1" longer than box 4. Using cardboard, spread glue on fabric; press onto side of box 4 so fabric extends evenly at top and bottom. Fold excess to inside; glue. Cut star fabric same size as bottom of box 4; glue in place. Cut star fabric 2" larger all around than lid 4. Glue fabric to lid. Fold excess to inside of lid; glue in place, clipping fabric as needed. Cut star fabric 2" wider than box 4 and 15" long. Turn under ¹/₂" on bottom and sides. Glue folded edges in place. Wrap and glue around box 4. Gather at top; glue edges.

Finishing: Stack boxes. Tie remaining ribbon in bow around top of cap.

Miss Holly (1 of 3)
1 square = 1"

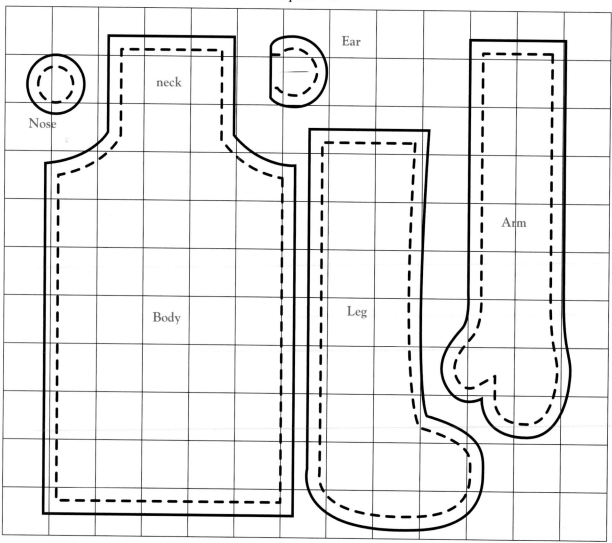

Nose · neck · Ear · Body · Leg · Arm

150

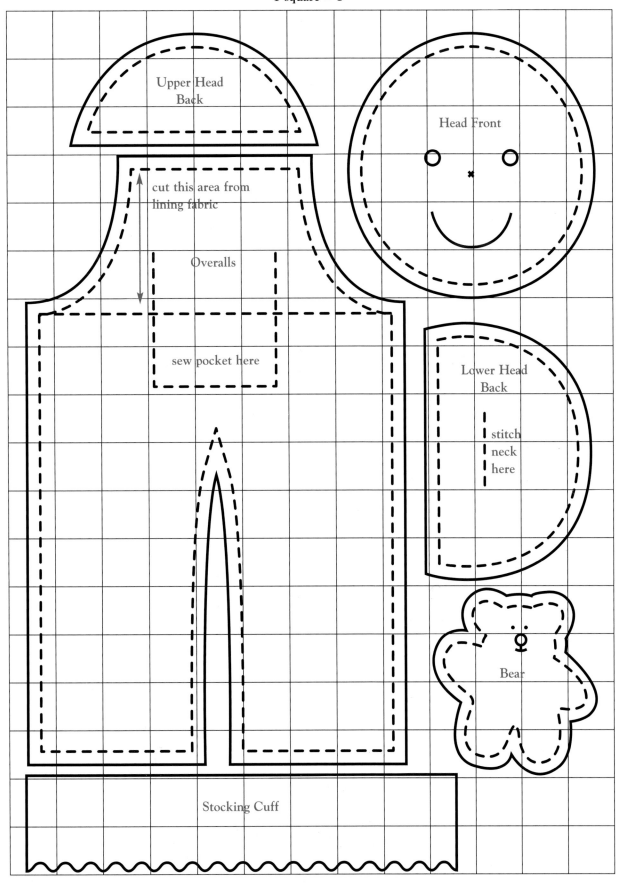

Upper Head Back

Head Front

cut this area from lining fabric

Overalls

sew pocket here

Lower Head Back

stitch neck here

Bear

Stocking Cuff

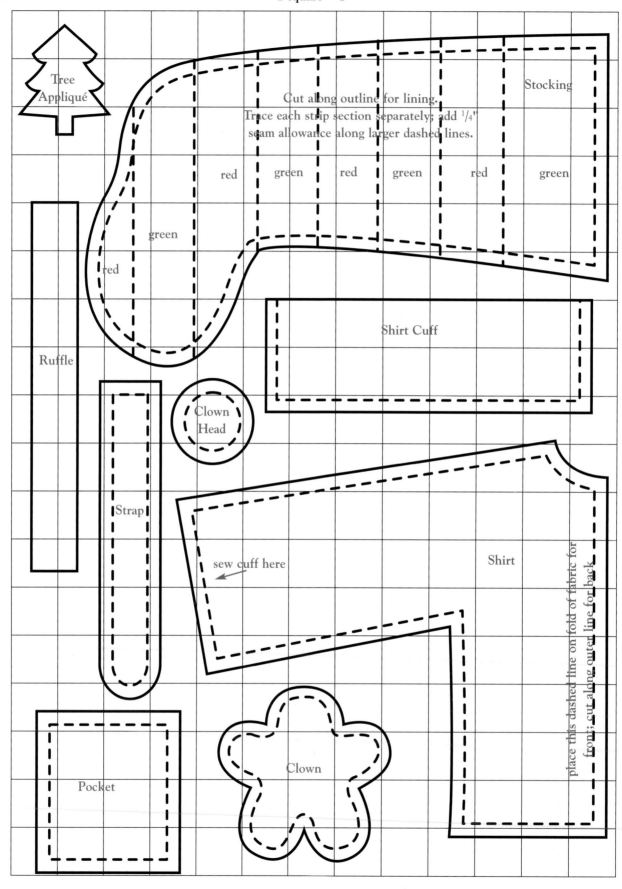

Tree Appliqué

Stocking

red   green   red   green   red   green

Cut along outline for lining.
Trace each strip section separately; add ¹/₄"
seam allowance along larger dashed lines.

green

red

Shirt Cuff

Ruffle

Clown Head

Strap

sew cuff here

Shirt

place this dashed line on fold of fabric for front; cut along outer line for back

Pocket

Clown

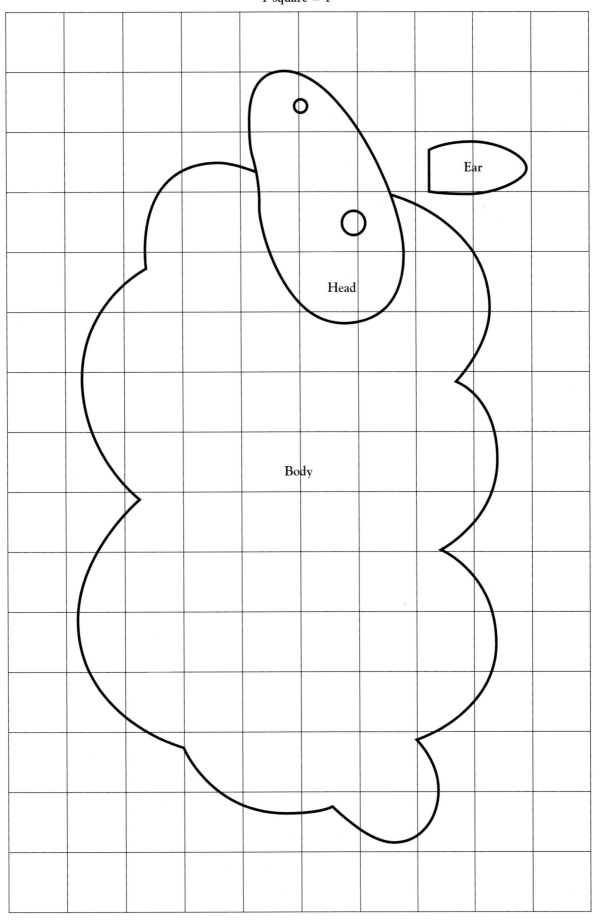

Ear

Head

Body

cookie countdown (pages 92-97)

Twelve Days of Cookies

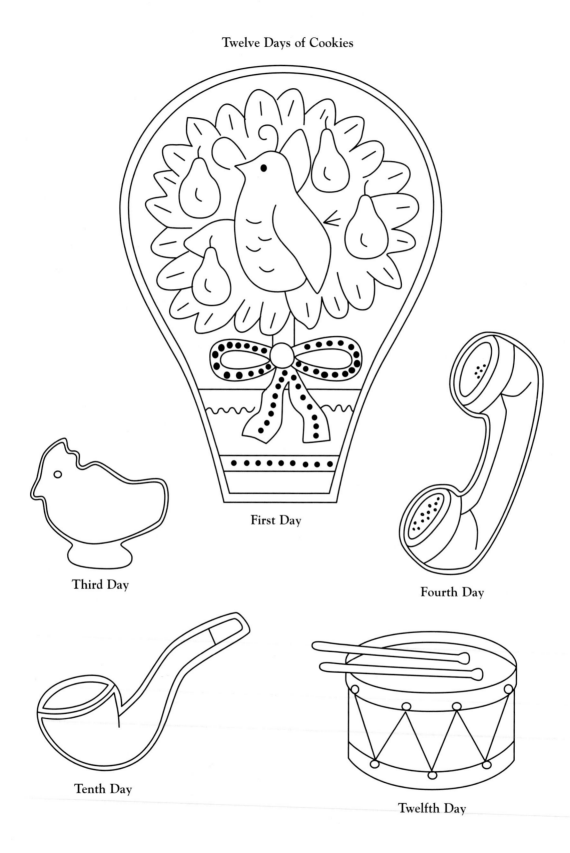

First Day

Third Day

Fourth Day

Tenth Day

Twelfth Day

basic how-to's

Embroidery

Backstitch

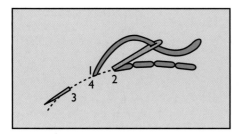

Cross Stitch

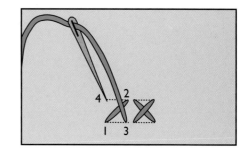

Blanket Stitch

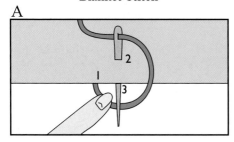

French Knot

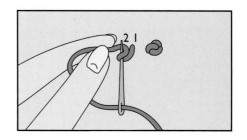

Satin Stitch

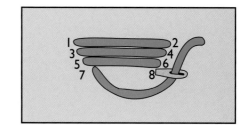

How to Enlarge Patterns

We recommend making enlargements on a copier –
it's fast and accurate. Use the "enlarge" button; repeat
copying and enlarging until you get the desired size.
For some patterns you may also use the
grid method: Copy the pattern one
square at a time onto 1" grid graph
paper to get a full-size pattern.

how-to's index

recipe index

credits

To Magna IV Color Imaging of Little Rock, Arkansas, we say thank you for the superb color reproduction and excellent pre-press preparation.

To the talented people who helped create the following projects and recipes in this book, we extend a special word of thanks:
- Art Accents: *Pen and Desk Set*, pg. 59.
- Samantha Bellucci: *Birdhouse Window Box*, pg. 14; *Star Ornaments*, pg. 17.
- Julia Bernstein: *Chicken-Wire Window Box*, pg. 15; *Colorful Tree Topper*, pg. 19; *Fabric-Covered Journals*, pg. 60.
- Joyce Tapply Bingham: *Sweater Mittens*, pg. 62.
- Brother International Corporation: *Monogrammed Stocking*, pg. 18.
- Janis Bullis: *Pocket Stocking, Lattice Stocking*, pg. 18.
- Mary Ellen Cocchi: *Trinket-Filled Soaps*, pg. 61.
- Diane Ferree for Art Accents: *Beaded Finials*, pg. 43.
- Lori Hellander: *Chenille Snowballs*, pg. 7; *Appliquéd Throw*, pg. 9; *Appliquéd Napkins*, pg. 11; *"Etched" Snowflake Glasses*, pg. 13; *Paper Votive Holders, Tin Cone Ornaments*, pg. 24; *Pinwheel Star and Ornaments*, pg. 25; *String Tag Garland*, pg. 27.
- Rob Hellander: *Silver Leaf Mirror*, pg. 10; *Jeweled Ornaments*, pg. 42; *Braided Topiaries*, pg. 45.
- Lauren Hunter: *Bottle Stoppers*, pg. 61.
- Luba Kierkosz: *Snowflake Tree Topper*, pg. 7; *Star Garland, Snowflake Place Mat*, pg. 11; *Lightbulb Place Cards*, pg. 45.
- Cheryl Kleinman: *Fondant Snowflakes and Place Card*, pg. 11.
- Karen Laurence: *Plaid Tablecloth, Ribbon Topiary*, pg. 21.
- Jan McDougal: *Fireplace Screen*, pg. 31.
- JoAnn Millett: *Sock Stocking*, pg. 53.
- Offray Ribbons: *Folded Ribbon Star*, pg. 42.
- Ann Pisa-Relli: *Extra-Brilliant Balls*, pg. 16.
- Pat Richards: *Holly Stocking*, pg. 53.
- Janet Rosell: *Pipe Cleaner Snowflakes*, pg. 7; *Looped Garland*, pg. 43.
- Rebecca Rosen: *Knitted Stocking*, pg. 18.
- Kathi Rubinstein: *Misty-Gray Stocking, Ice-Blue Stocking, Regal Blue Stocking*, pg. 8.
- Roy Rudin: *Organza Tree Skirt*, pg. 40; *Patchwork Tree Skirt*, pg. 51.
- Daphne A. Shirley: *Ball Ornaments*, pg. 26; *Paper Cone Ornaments*, pg. 27; *Ribbon-Wrapped Goody Boxes*, pg. 30; *Decoupaged Mitten Box*, pg. 49; *Ribbon Ball Ornaments*, pg. 50.
- Sarah Shirley: *Cone Ornaments*, pg. 24; *3-D Paper Ornaments*, pg. 27; *Tree Skirt*, pg. 28; *Scarf Stocking*, pg. 29; *Joy Pillows*, pg. 31.
- Deborah Spencer for The Warm Company: *Mock Chenille Stocking*, pg. 29.
- Robin Tarnoff: *Victorian Skater*, pg. 6; *Mini Skates*, pg. 12; *Miss Holly Doll*, pg. 63.
- Chris Wallace: *Mr. and Mrs. Claus Boxes*, pg. 65.
- Brooke Warberg: *Ribbon-Wrapped Bags*, pg. 30.
- Jim Williams: *Holiday Stockings*, pg. 44; *Gift Package Place Mats*, pg. 45; *Heart Ornaments*, pg. 50; *Patchwork Stocking, Ladybug Stocking*, pg. 53; *Chair-Back Heart*, pg. 54; *Napping Mat and Pillow*, pg. 65.
- And of course, special thanks to the expertise of the *Family Circle* Food Department.

Special acknowledgment is given to the following *Family Circle* photographers:
- Antonis Achilleos: bottom right, pg. 56; top left, pg. 57; pg. 63; left, pg. 71; pgs. 72, 73, 75, 92, 93, 109.
- Mary Ellen Bartley: pgs. 86, 88-91.
- John Bessler: center left, pg. 39; pgs. 48-54; top right, pg. 56; center, pg. 59; pg. 65.
- David Bishop: right, pg. 68.
- Monica Buck: right, pg. 39; pgs. 40-42; top, page 43; pg. 44; bottom, pg. 45; right, pg. 57.
- Steve Cohen: pgs. 104, 105.
- Francine Fleischer: pg. 14; top left, pg. 15.
- Tria Giovan: pg. 33.
- Lydia Gould: center left, pg. 47.
- Brian Hagiwara: pgs. 17, 18; right, pg. 20; top, pg. 37; top center, pg. 47; pgs. 67, 70; right, pg. 71; pgs. 82, 84, 85; pgs. 100, 107, 108; bottom, pg. 110.
- Paul Kopelow: right, pg. 23.
- Kit Latham: bottom, pg. 15.
- Kevin Lein: pgs. 6-13; center, pg. 23; top right, pg. 38.
- Michael Luppino: pgs. 16, 19; left, pg. 20; pg. 21; bottom, pg. 34.
- Nadia MacKenzie: top, pg. 55.
- Steven Mays: pgs. 24-29; pgs. 30, 31; bottom, pg. 37; bottom, pg. 38; top, pg. 59.
- Josh McHugh: bottom, pg. 59; pg. 74.
- Jeff McNamara: bottom, pg. 39.
- Steven Mark Needham: pg. 66.
- Dean Powell: pg. 64.
- Alan Richardson: top, pg. 34; top left, pg. 47; pg. 62; left, pg. 68; pgs. 76-81; pgs. 94-99; pgs. 102, 103; pgs. 106, 109; top, pg. 110; pgs. 111-113; pg. 115.
- Carin Riley: bottom left, pg. 57.
- George Ross: pg. 69.
- Joseph Scafuro: pgs. 60, 61.
- Mark Thomas: pg. 101.
- Ross Whitaker: top, center and bottom left, pg. 56.
- Reprinted from *Country Christmas*. Available from Lorenz Books, NY: pg. 46; bottom left, pg. 47.

We also wish to thank the following *Family Circle* photography stylists:
- Betty Alfenito: pgs. 73, 75; top, pg. 110.
- Denise Canter: pgs. 98, 99, 102, 111, 115.
- Cathy Cook: pgs. 82, 84, 85, 92, 93, 101, 104, 105, 106.
- Ann Dixon: right, pg. 68.
- Trish Foley: pgs. 76-81.
- Robyn Glaser: pgs. 86, 88-91.
- Scott Gordon: top right, pg. 38.
- Edward Kemper Design: top, pg. 34; left, pg. 68; pgs. 69, 72, 103, 109, 112, 113.
- Christine McCabe: pgs. 67, 100, 107, 108.
- Faith Meade: pg. 70; right, pg. 71.
- Janet Rosell: pgs. 6-13.

Thanks also go to the following *Family Circle* food stylists:
- Baked Ideas: Cookies #4, #10, #12, pgs. 94-97.
- A. J. Battifarano: pg. 70; right, pg. 71; pgs. 76-82, 84, 85, 107, 108.
- Roscoe Betsill: pgs. 86, 88-91.
- Cathy Cook: pgs. 73, 75, 82, 84, 85, 92, 93, 101, 104, 105, 106.
- Kevin Crafts: left, pg. 68; pgs. 69, 103.
- Anne Disrude: pg. 100; top, pg. 110.
- Susan Ehlich: pgs. 104, 105.
- Rick Ellis: pgs. 98, 99, 102, 111.
- Brett Kurzweil: right, pg. 68.
- William Smith: pgs. 72, 106, 112, 113, 115.
- Andrea B. Swenson: pg. 67, Cookies #1, #7, #11, pgs. 94-97.
- Karen Tack: pgs. 74, 92, 93; Cookies #2, #3, #5, #6, #8, #9, pgs. 94-97; pg. 109.
- Fred Thompson: pg. 101.

We want to especially thank Leisure Arts photographer Larry Pennington of Pennington Studios in Little Rock, Arkansas, for his excellent work.